SURRENDER WITH MEHER BABA

Laurent Weichberger
& Companions

Praise for Surrender with Meher Baba

Intelligent Surrender.

Yes, intelligent surrender .... can be forgiveness. And can be trust, and can be love. This exceptional book -- in many ways -- goes into the ability, a process, to change in a way that your sinew and heart not only may want, but are destined to. All things are a divine Rose that needs to fully open, and will from evolution's embrace. The profound, astounding claim of who Meher Baba says he is, in a way, inherently keeps him separate from the world ... from the average
discerning mind.

To me, the World Teachers are voted into their vital, vital roles. That is, is it not the case: That millions have heard the name Jesus, and then something in their mind or soul said: Check him out. And when they do they might in some way say -- "He ain't jiving." "He is part of the real deal." "Hell, he is really like the SUN."

And then, dear Buddha could get the same "thumbs up," to the extent that one also even tries to: "Sit until you know." As seems the path of most all the Great Ones. And Rama was there, and Krishna, and Muhammad and Zoroaster.

And I am giving ten to one odds on any bets, that over the next 100 years or so: Many, many in the world will come to feel about Meher Baba as Laurent Weichberger so intimately and remarkably speaks about him in this grand, significant, wonderful book.

This book will help you cast for a vote for your True Self, and in doing so lessen your pain.

Daniel Ladinsky,
International bestselling Penguin Random House author

Surrender with Meher Baba

By Laurent Weichberger & Companions

Published by OmPoint Press
First Edition August 2020
Second Printing September 6, 2020

Cover photo courtesy of MSI Collection,
Grateful appreciation to Martin and Christine Cook for all they do.

Cover and interior design by Karl Moeller

Bodoni Svty Two 12 point type

ISBN 978-0-578-73804-8

This book is dedicated with all my love to my son Cyprus,
just as I rededicate and surrender my life to
Avatar Meher Baba.

"Through unfathomable ways, I lead you to liberation.
Accept My rhythm, come in tune with it without reservations.
My rhythm of Truth shall redeem you;
It will open your heart,
it will give you new love."

Meher Baba

Mehera J. Irani, Baba's Beloved, is seen leaning over Avatar Meher Baba, resting in a hammock during a picnic near Arangaon on May 1, 1937. Margaret Craske bears witness to their love (on the right). Photo most likely by Elizabeth Patterson.

Foreword

Evie Lindemann

For those potential readers who might take a dive into this book on the topic of surrender, some of what you may discover will surprise you and some of the content will be familiar. Meher Baba, in his writings, reminds us that the spiritual path is unique to each individual. He also places emphasis on the relinquishment of the ego as a necessary step along the spiritual path. Here, with his skillful inquiry, Laurent shows us how Meher Baba wades into the waters of surrender with full confidence that the spiritual aspirant, over time, will recognize both the difficulty and the inherent value in taking steps toward surrender.

Basic questions, such as how, when, why, and who will embark on the process of surrender are explored in the first half of this book by Laurent, with generous quotes from Meher Baba. Laurent's love for Meher Baba shines through each page, as he explains his understanding of the path Baba has laid out for us. Laurent also invites us to consider what the obstacles to surrender are, how surrender must be an active rather than a passive process, and why surrender must be sincerely executed. The gap between Meher Baba's words and how we interpret them and integrate them into our daily lives is explored by Laurent in Part I of the book as well as by additional spiritual writing companions through personal stories and poetry in Part II of the book.

All of the nuances and obstacles regarding the process of surrender and its end lead us to two simple yet profound truths. The first is that our journey reveals that we never were separate; rather "You and I are not we but one" always was, is, and forever will be the ultimate reality. The experience of Oneness is the goal. Our difficulties in the world provide us with the steppingstones to practice acts of surrender on a daily basis, and to gradually make our way to the door of the infinite embrace.

Prologue

Laurent Weichberger

It is impossible for me to separate my journey with surrender from my journey with Avatar Meher Baba. It is difficult to explain just how intertwined faith and surrender truly are for me, and I believe many others. Whether it is Christ, Allah, Buddha, or another spiritual master having a guide on this journey is paramount as it takes you out of your own wants and desires and pushes you to achieve something better. For those readers who are unfamiliar with Meher Baba let me take this opportunity to provide a brief introduction.

I found Meher Baba in the Spring of 1986 and came to understand Meher Baba as the most recent incarnation of the Avatar, God in Human form. Born Merwan Sheriar Irani in Pune, India in 1894 he too went on a journey of enlightenment with the aid of five spiritual masters. Meher Baba inspired thousands during his lifetime and a thriving community still persists to this day. There are a myriad of sources available for more in depth information on the life and teachings of Avatar Meher Baba, but here I will speak more to my personal journey with him and what he has taught me in my own life.

Table of Contents

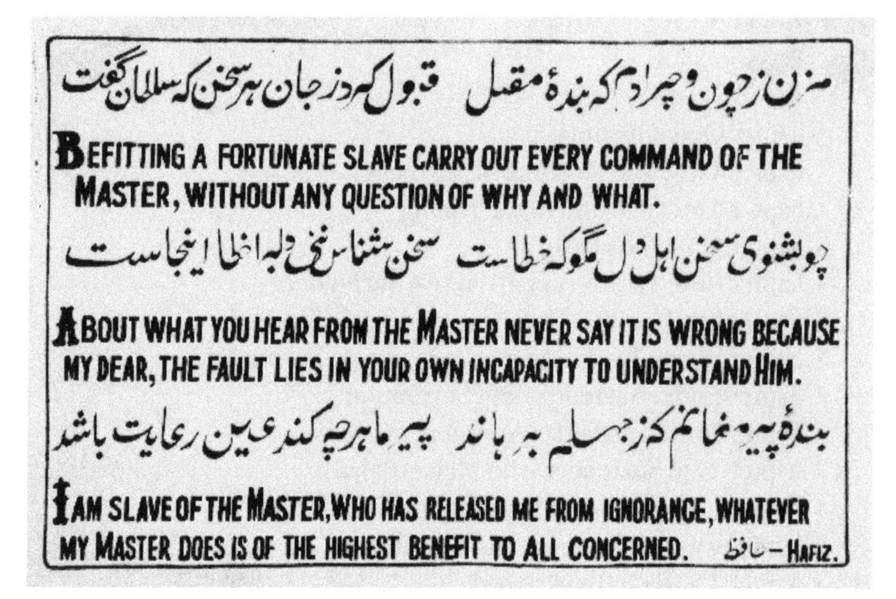

مزن ز چون و چرا دم که بنده مقبل   قبول کرد به جان هر سخن که سلطان گفت

BEFITTING A FORTUNATE SLAVE CARRY OUT EVERY COMMAND OF THE MASTER, WITHOUT ANY QUESTION OF WHY AND WHAT.

چو بشنوی سخن اهل دل مگو که خطاست   سخن شناس نئی دلبرا خطا اینجاست

ABOUT WHAT YOU HEAR FROM THE MASTER NEVER SAY IT IS WRONG BECAUSE MY DEAR, THE FAULT LIES IN YOUR OWN INCAPACITY TO UNDERSTAND HIM.

بندهٔ پیر مغانم که ز جهلم برهاند   پیر ما هر چه کند عین رعایت باشد

I AM SLAVE OF THE MASTER, WHO HAS RELEASED ME FROM IGNORANCE, WHATEVER MY MASTER DOES IS OF THE HIGHEST BENEFIT TO ALL CONCERNED. حافظ – HAFIZ.

I was told that the last words which Meher Baba had read out loud before he passed away on January 31, 1969 was this poem from the great poet and spiritual master, Hafiz. [1]

Chapter One: Opening

"Understanding has no meaning.
Love has meaning. Obedience has more meaning.
Holding of my daaman has the most meaning."
Meher Baba[2]

Introduction

The opening quote from Meher Baba seems to be a great way to introduce the subject of surrender for those who may not have spent a lot of time with this word perhaps other than maybe in the traditional sense of flying the white flag, with your hands up in the air. Surrender, from a spiritual point of view, is much different than a military surrender or strategic admission of defeat.

As I was just writing this in a coffee shop in Charlotte, North Carolina, Bob Marley came on the radio singing, "Is this love?" Perhaps Baba is reminding me to start this whole book with the relationship between Surrender and Love, instead of the dictionary definition and old-fashioned views of surrender.

The Merriam-Webster Dictionary says:

Surrender :
1a : to yield to the power, control, or possession of another upon compulsion or demand
b : to give up completely or agree to forgo especially in favor of another
2a : to give (oneself) up into the power of another especially as a prisoner
b : to give (oneself) over to something (such as an influence)[3]

However, the dictionary was never intended to be a spiritual book. It is simply how people commonly use the word surrender. Let's go deeper and tackle this whole question of surrender, or, "giving oneself over," from the point of view of the limited false ego, giving itself over to something "higher," or more spiritual, or divine. Let's see where Baba takes us, and what this all means.

Baba said, "Understanding has no meaning." For example, one may understand that using drugs is harmful, physically, mentaly and spiritually, and yet still continue to use the drugs. So, what is the value of the understanding? He continued that, "Love has meaning." When you begin to love someone, or something, other than yourself, it is meaningful progress in the right direction. Apparently this loving leads to something greater, but to what? Many people are capable of amazing things when inspired by love, and one could even say that for most the spiritual path begins with loving.[4]

Baba stated, "Obedience has more meaning." So, in our analogy and in the spiritual realm, Baba is speaking of obeying God, or one's personal Spiritual Master. Such obedience came from the love bond established between the Master and disciple, and in Baba's view obedience is greater than love itself. In our story, perhaps we can say obeying the Master's guidance, not to use drugs, is vastly superior to understanding the need to stop using drugs. So, through love one may gather the strength to obey. And after a time of loving and obeying the Master, it goes even deeper into surrender.

In love there is a lover and a Beloved. In obedience there is Master (giving an order) and disciple, obeying the instruction. In surrender, the lover and the Beloved move into a closer dance, a slow intimate dance, and there is a sense of anticipating the need before the order or wish is ever spoken. Knowing each other so well, there is a movement of love, a dynamic obedience, and ineffable surrender. This silence transforms the whole situation, as then it is not really obedience, it is all unspoken, or internalized loving, mixed with some degree of bliss of the nearness of God. There is a sense of striving, but it is not for any self gain, as it is all to please the Beloved. This is what I have learned from over thirty years with Meher Baba.

Lastly, we see Baba gave us the somewhat enigmatic statement, "Holding of my daaman has the most meaning." Daaman literally means the hem of a garment, and so we need to go beyond the material sense of this phrase. Enigmatic, because many not familiar with Baba will not know what he means by this, and even those in the Meher Baba community may struggle to interpret this image in light of it being more important than obeying Baba. So what does it mean? To put it plainly, it means surrender. Why do I say that? Because elsewhere Baba explained holding on to his daaman as meaning – like a child who holds fast to the hem of the skirt of mother in the marketplace, so as not to be lost or wander off, so, hold fast to Baba and don't be distracted by the illusions of the world, the Maya all around, tempting, enticing, entrapping. Also, while holding to the hem of the mother's garment, we cannot use our hands (or wander off with our feet), to get into other troubles.

One of the last things that Meher Baba's beloved Mehera J. Irani was told by Baba, on January 31, 1969, shortly before he passed away, was simply "Be brave." As fate would have it, she lived bravely from that day until her passing in 1989, twenty years later. What her bravery entailed only she can tell. However, I met her in India, and I can testify to her loving, caring, sometimes sharp, presence and how she continued to serve Baba - from her front porch, by sharing her wisdom and love with all who gathered to hear from her about Baba. It was truly inspiring.

I remember once when I was praying, I asked myself, when I pray – Why do I fold my hands in front of my chest (in the typical Western prayer style)? Naturally, because that is what I saw modeled by others all of my life, but I wanted to go deeper, and discover the meaning in this gesture. My intuition said that when I pray in that manner, I am showing Baba (or

God) – Look I am here with you, focused on you, not doing anything, I am just being with you. My hands are symbolic of doing in the world, and of my work. If I stop working, and stop doing, I can be. As God said to King David of the Jews, "Be still, and know that I am God."[5]

And how do we hold fast to Meher Baba's daaman, how do we surrender to this extent? It just occurred to me that Baba has the image of two hands again in this, "holding his daaman," and perhaps he is keeping us busy holding on to him between prayers. The thought, "How do we do all of this?" is the primary subject of this book, with a bit of who, what, where, when, and why mixed in.

In the Spring of 1986, when I was seventeen years old, and not long after recovering from the deep shock of my father's suicide, I started down the path of loving Avatar Meher Baba. At that time, I had just seen Baba's photo for the first time. It was printed on the inside of the 1964 Universal Message, by Meher Baba that was given out at the World's Fair in New York. [6] This message was shared with me by Michael Mathias, with Patty and Doug Stalker at a coffee shop in Manhattan. It was maybe a few months after this introduction to Baba, that I was encouraged to visit the Meher Spiritual Center in Myrtle Beach, South Carolina. I was told to write to the center, and request a retreat there. In response to my request, a man named David Silverman wrote back to me confirming my reservation. In his loving letter he included a "Baba card," which is a little card, like the old baseball cards (without the stats), showing a photo of Meher Baba, and some words from him. I read the little card with interest, and admired the photo of Baba on it, and still clearly remember this quote from him:

> "If you make me your real Father, all differences and contentions between you, and all personal problems in connection with your lives, will become dissolved in the Ocean of my love." [7]

I was standing in the upstairs of my Manhattan apartment, in my bedroom, and as I held the little card, right after reading Baba's words, I said to Baba out loud, "Okay Baba, I am making you my Real Father." Little did I know, but that was actually a giant turning point in my life, and perhaps the first real surrender on my spiritual path back to him.

Chapter Two: The Meaning of Surrender

"Holy is the fire between your will and ours,
in which we are refined."
Leonard Cohen [1]

"Surrender with Meher Baba" means to give up completely what I want and desire, to forgo my plan for my life, in favor of what my Spiritual Master, Avatar Meher Baba, wants for me, and has planned for me. In other words, if I am attached to what I want, I don't leave room for him to guide me to what is best for me. My desires create resistance to his guidance.

When people would argue with Baba's spiritual guidance, rather than arguing with them he would frequently respond with the phrase, "Please yourself."

Ultimately, as Baba explained, what is best for me is Self-realization. This is the path he has laid out for me, step by step. So, I can either walk my own path, that is the path of self-will and ego-centric desires, or I can walk the spiritual path of self-effacement, self-giving love, God's wish and will for me, and what He wants. This is, I believe, also the meaning of the statement from Mani, Baba's sister. It all adds up to the same thing.

This is most likely the single most difficult thing I can aspire to as a human being, as it goes against the very grain of all that I have been taught in this world, and it is antithetical to my inheritance of lust-anger-greed based on countless sub-human forms in my journey of evolution of consciousness. I will dive more deeply into this, in the chapter Surrender with Meher Baba later in this volume.

What is Surrender?

Beyond dictionary definitions there is the spiritual notion of surrender. This has nothing to do with raising your hands in the air, and passively submitting. This is an active engagement with the Will of God, and a disengagement with self-will. In other words, in order to understand what is spiritual surrender, we have to understand what is not surrender, or the opposite of surrender. The opposite of spiritual surrender is the ego-centric life which seeks at every opportunity to fulfill desires. The man of the world, who has no interest in spiritual living, is consumed by desires, and their fulfillment, and the list is long. More money, more sex, more and better food and drink. A better position at work, more power. A shorter list is something like, lust, greed, pride, and anger. If the worldly values are like that, then the spiritual values must be more like love, generosity, tolerance (acceptance), and forgiveness. This means, ultimately, that one who can surrender self-will, gradually, will live more and more in love, peace, and acceptance of others. Ultimately living more and more in alignment with God's Will.

According to Baba, the entire spiritual path is a series of surrenders, as he says: "Spiritual advancement is a succession of one surrender after another until the goal of the final surrenderance of the separate ego-life is completely achieved." [2]

This point was brought home to me recently by the wondrous poet Leonard Cohen, who responded to an interviewer's question, "We sense that there is a will that is behind all things, and we're also aware of our own will, and it is the distance between those two wills that creates the mystery that we call religion. It is the attempt to reconcile our will with another will that we can't quite put our finger on, but we feel is powerful and existent. It's the space between those two wills that creates our predicament." [3] The prayer given by Jesus, known as "The Lord's Prayer" has this line, "Thy will be done, on Earth as it is in Heaven." [4]

From this line we can see that in Heaven where the angels abide with the Lord, God's will is being done. This prayer is asking that God's will should prevail on Earth as well. Well, it can prevail on Earth, if we surrender, and replace our self-will with God's Will. This is at least one meaning of surrender, the active effort to sublimate the selfish desires, in favor of what we are perceiving is the wish and the will of God. Naturally, this is a difficult process, as it goes against the nature of the mind, the ego, and the ways of the world (worldly values). Another saying we have heard many times is to "be in the world, but not of the world." For years, I pondered the meaning of this phrase. I think I am starting to understand that it is all about values. How am I living up to my spiritual values? If I am forgiving, loving, kind, generous, and patient, I am not of this world, but striving for the angelic values, God's values.

When Jesus was praying in the Garden of Gethsemane, shortly before his betrayal by Judas and then his crucifixion, he prayed to God, "Father, if you are willing, take this cup from me; yet not my will, but yours be done." [5] What does this saying from Jesus mean? Was he really praying to God the Father? Well, earlier in the gospel stories, Jesus reveals that he is one with his Father in Heaven. [6]

So praying to the Father, when he is already one with that Father doesn't make a lot of sense – unless, he is modeling behavior for us, and showing the world how to behave when praying to God. In that case, it makes perfect sense, because he is basically saying, in this scripture – God, please take away this suffering, but only if it is your will. He is surrendering his self-will to the Divine Will. Then, when remembering this, we too can participate in this surrender. When we suffer, we too can pray to God, please take away this suffering, not in accordance with my will, but may thy will be done my Lord.

Let's remember that Jesus as the Christ, only says or does everything for others. As the Christ (Avatar) he is already One with the Father, so his actions and words are to benefit humanity, and all of creation. To me, this is obviously Christ exemplifying what it means to give over self-will to God's Will. On the other hand, and this is the divine mystery, Jesus was also a Jewish man named "Yeshua" who had a human form, human energy, a human thinking mind, and one can imagine human feelings as well. What part of him was speaking to God? This is worthy of meditation and contemplation.

Who Surrenders?

This may seem self evident, however, if we take a quick inventory of the possibilities, we can see there are some options here. Let's examine some possibilities. Is it the mind with its thoughts and ideas that surrenders? Is it the heart with its feelings and emotions? Is it the soul which surrenders? Is it the ego of the individual? Is it the body? Is it the energy of a person? Is it the spirit? What is the difference between all these aspects anyway?

What is the ego? In Latin, "ego" literally means "I" as in, "me, myself, and I." So it is the sense of self as distinct from the divine self. Different people seem to identify with other aspects of self, such as the body, or the mind. Some people such as those on a spiritual path are actively trying to subdue their ego. Some people identify with their energy. Some think of the spirit, or the soul. What is it that survives death, and reincarnates?

In my observations of my own spiritual life, the ego, which consciously and willingly associates with a genuine Spiritual Master, or the Avatar (Christ), or some aspect of God, starts to realize that living an ego-centric life of desire fulfillment is not going to bring lasting happiness and satisfaction, and starts to experiment with self-giving, loving, and serving, and this gradually leads to love, obedience and ultimately surrender. So, the limited ego self, the personality of the spiritual aspirant, becomes more and more willing to let go, and trust God, and literally surrender that to which it had been clinging, and trying to control through self-will. But when does this process start?

Chapter Three: Divine Right Timing

"In the silence of your perfect surrender, my love which is always silent can flow to you – to be yours always to keep and to share with those who seek me. When the Word of my love breaks out of its silence and speaks in your hearts, telling you who I really am, you will know that that is the Real Word you have been always longing to hear." [1]
Meher Baba

From my limited observations, and understanding, it seems that most human beings only start the surrender process when they have tried everything else, and found no satisfaction in life. This reminds me of the people who say they were looking for their keys in their house, and the keys are always in the last place they look. That sounds so funny to me, because it would have to be that way, unless they kept looking after finding their keys. But in the case of the spiritual aspirant, regardless of their religion, it seems the final aspect of the spiritual path, after the honeymoon, the excitement, the ardour, and the deep contemplation and wisdom sharing, is the need to surrender the false self, the ego life, for the life of love in God.

I believe one must be willing to lose everything in the process of surrenderance to the Divine, and with my experience of life, this is somewhat terrifying. There is a not-knowing what will happen if I am successful in surrender. Maybe that is why I surrender in baby-steps along the path. And beyond the failure or success of this process, there are many other questions which arise. That's okay, it doesn't all have to be crystal clear and brightly lit up to take these surrender steps. I give myself permission – to walk along towards the One, in darkness, in uncertainty. When I first came to Baba, as a teen, my Baba contact Michael introduced me to the poet Rainer Maria Rilke, whose poetry and other writings I immediately loved. One of his saying comes to mind here:

"Be patient toward all that is unsolved in your heart and try to love the questions themselves, like locked rooms and like books that are now written in a very foreign tongue. Do not now seek the answers, which cannot be given you because you would not be able to live them. And the point is, to live everything. Live the questions now. Perhaps you will then gradually, without noticing it, live along some distant day into the answer."

Where do we Surrender?

It seems to me that the only real answer to this question, "Where do we surrender?" is in daily life. Spiritually in daily life seems to have no past and only a misty idea of a future. All the real work seems to be happening in each Now. And "the now" can only be found in daily living.

Of course, the stereotype is that one must remove oneself from the world, and find some secluded place, like a cave or monastery, or retreat to be spiritual. But the new paradigm, and the one Meher Baba recommends, is to stay in the world, and live your spiritual life as it comes, day by day. There is no special place, or sacred time, other than right here and right now. In fact, this type of practical spirituality is more difficult than going off to a temple or sacred space, and can be rich with opportunities. Perhaps we can say that we surrender here in daily life, and it is the offering from the ego, in the heart, to God.

How do we Surrender?

This question – is a little like the question posed by a man to Meher Baba in 1964, about repeating God's name as a way of loving him and coming closer to the Truth.

Baba responded:

> "Do you love your wife?"
>
> "Yes, Baba. I love her very much."
>
> "What would you do if she were staying far away from you?"
>
> "I would remember her, of course."
>
> "Would you remember her with a rosary in your hand? Would you sit in a corner and repeat her name?"
>
> "No, I would think about her spontaneously with love."
>
> Baba stated, "In the same way, automatic remembrance of God in a natural way is what is worthwhile. And without love, it is not possible. When there is intense thirst for the remembrance of the Beloved, love is born, and one's only thought is of the Beloved. "[2]

There are countless souls in the world, and all have their own unique relationship with God, in whatever aspect – personal as those who follow Meher Baba, or another spiritual master. Some resonate more with the impersonal, the formless infinite aspect of God, such as the Jewish, Sufi, Christian God in the Beyond (sometimes called the Divine Father or Divine Mother), or any other aspect of God. We can say that each person must find their own personal way to surrender. When the divine relationship is strong, and fueled by higher love, we can see that it naturally leads to surrender.

For example, when I imagine a conversation between the Franciscan Brother Leo and Saint Francis of Assisi, I can easily imagine how and why Leo would surrender to Francis as a spiritual master. Likewise with Lakshman's surrender to his own brother, Lord Ram, as described in the

Ramayana. Prince Ram, as the Avatar, is banished from his own kingdom for fourteen years into the wilderness, and his closest brother Lakshman, also a prince, decides to give up the royal life to accompany his brother and protect him. Such love is truly inspiring, and yet isn't that depth of relationship beyond love? He obeyed Ram and served him for the rest of his life. [3]

Even without the divine relationship being in human form, such a spiritual bond can span lifetimes and inspire deep love, obedience and surrender. Such was the case with the Hindu Saint Mira's surrender to Lord Krishna, and St. Francis' relationship with Jesus Christ. As Meher Baba explained,

> "Mira was not born at the time when Krishna manifested himself as the Avatar in human form. Even then her love surpassed that of the gopis. In this sense her love is unique, unparalleled. The same can be said about Francis of Assisi's love for Jesus Christ. He had not seen Jesus physically but his love for Christ excelled that of Peter, the Rock. Because Francis never met Jesus, his longing and love were that much greater." [4]

Saint Francis: An Example of Complete Surrender to God's Love

In discussing the life of Saint Francis with my wife Vanessa, and our Italian friend Tommaso Mini, a few points came up which deserve special attention. Initially, Vanessa reminded me of the relationship Francis had with his father and of his year in a dungeon as a prisoner of war. However, I tended to focus more on the dramatic ending of Francis' story and his experience of stigmata. Before we dive deeply into these points, let's remember that Baba explained that Francis was a unique example, saying, "Saint Francis of Assisi was the only one of the very few saints in the West to become a Perfect Master." [5]

Now to discover more about the surrenders which suffuse his extraordinary life with God. One could easily look at Francis' entire life as a series of surrenders, and make a book of just that. But for this chapter, these are some great examples.

In the first story, Francis has been captured during a local war with neighboring Perugia. Vanessa shared, "This event was a dividing moment between Francis' privileged life as a youth and his adult life as a conscious adult striving to love God where he abandons dreams of knighthood, chivalry, and boyhood adventures. Francis returns to Assisi having spent a year in a dungeon where he contracted malaria. His weakened state, physically and mentally, along with his illness which stretched on even after his ransomed release, was an experience that drew Francis inward towards his spiritual life where peace, justice and true poverty became his aspirations."

In the second story, Francis and his father are arguing outside the church of Assisi, because of Francis' misdeeds, and his father's desire for a fitting punishment. The priest is called out to pass judgment, before the entire town, and in a twist of fate, Francis takes the opportunity to strip naked, and putting all his belongings on the ground in front of his father, says - "I am no longer your son, you are no longer my father..." and walked off alone into the woods, never again to belong to his own family. When I discussed this with Vanessa, and also Tommaso, a Baba-lover and native Italian, and knowing the Italian culture and family values, I asked - How would that have been perceived by a Thirteenth Century Italian?

Tommaso said it would have been, "Beyond shocking... and unheard of..." because at that time, Francis lived an extremely privileged life, the son of a merchant. He was thereby renouncing his privilege and his family, at the same time. This would be a surrender of any connection to the family name, and inheritance to come, as well as a present moment surrender of all the attachments and access to home, food, and clothing. This was not a public "show," for dramatic affect, it was a deep turning point for Francis, and an expression of his soul. Francis began to embrace Lady Poverty, as he would later explain. From that day onward, Francis would rely wholly and solely on God. This was both an internal and an external renunciation and profound surrender which would launch Francis into his spiritual adventure.

I am reminded of this part of the "Song of the New Life" by Meher Baba and Dr. Abdul Ghani:

> If you are serious about living this New Life,
> Then wholeheartedly renounce this ephemeral existence.
> We have taken to this life, in which we rely only on God;
> In this, our will (to do or die) is strengthened by the oath taken;
> We merrily sing the song of hopelessness;
> We invite all calamities and difficulties. [6]

La Verna, Italy. There is now a church built over the exact spot where Francis prayed in seclusion, atop this cliff face on the left, and received stigmata. Photo by Vanessa Weichberger.

Lastly we will discuss one of Francis' last spiritual experiences (two years before his death) during 1224 C.E., and what I think of as his final surrender. At this point in his life, he is about forty-three years old, and he makes a special trip to Mount La Verna, to fast and pray alone. I have been to La Verna and I know this mountain. The spot where Francis prayed in seclusion is at the top of a sharp cliff face, and would have been extraordinarily remote. It is remote even today. He made a small camp with a few of the brothers in his order, and then removed himself, to be alone with God.

According to the stigmata legend, as recorded in *The Little Flowers of St. Francis*, [7] a book Baba had read out to him, and on which he commented, Francis earnestly prayed to share in the suffering of Jesus Christ. To me this prayer, of wanting to share Christ's burden is a mystical surrender. Life is difficult for many. I see and find many who are suffering, physically, emotionally, mentally, energetically, and spiritually. This is, according to Baba, a result of their decisions, their karma, their desires, in short – the human condition. So, for an Italian saint to ask for more suffering, and not just more but the suffering that the Christ bears for humanity, to help him bear that cross for all, is not only amazing, but is the height of love and surrender.

During this prayer on the mountain, an angel appeared in the sky. This angel then inflicted Francis with wounds of stigmata – pierced in hands, feet, and side in the manner of Christ crucified. The resulting experience was, according to Baba, the culmination of Self-realization in Francis, and when he became a Perfect Master (Sadguru, or Qutub). My daughter Aspen reminded me to explain what a "Perfect Master" is, for those who may be new to this spiritual title, so I will do that now. According to Meher Baba, when any soul is reunited with Beloved God in conscious union and becomes Self-realized (or God-realized), that soul is able to know all, do all, and has the experience of infinite bliss. Some of those souls, who have such an experience come back into the gross world of Creation consciousness to help the souls who are still bound by ignorance to reach the same level they have attained. Such a master, when they have a circle of disciples and return to the world to help those in need are known as Perfect Masters, because they are spiritually perfect. They are one with the Truth, and they have nothing left to gain for themselves. They only exist to help others. According to Baba they help their circles of disciples first, as top priority, and next they help humanity. Back to the discussion of Saint Francis, and how he could have been God-realized... This detailed explanation came from a question asked by Don Stevens to Baba in Myrtle Beach during 1956:

> Don asked, "Baba, you have explained in the *Discourses*, *God Speaks* and elsewhere that an individual cannot attain God-realization without the aid of a living Perfect Master. Since there was no Perfect Master in the West at that time, how did Saint Francis achieve Realization?" Baba turned to Ivy and asked, "Have you heard of the ancient Sufi prophet, Khwaja Khizr?" She replied that she had heard Rabia Martin speak of him. Baba explained: "Khwaja Khizr now and then takes on a physical body if there is some spiritual situation that absolutely demands it. The Realization of Francis was such a case, because he had no Perfect Master to give him Realization. So on the night we read about on Mount La Verna, [near] Assisi, during which Saint Francis also received the stigmata [wounds of the Crucified Christ], Khwaja Khizr, in his temporary human form, gave this beloved Western saint the touch of grace which made him a Perfect Soul – a Sadguru or Perfect Master."[8]

What we know from St. Francis and his report to St. Claire and his order of monks, was that on La Verna he received the stigmata from an angel. What we hear from Baba, hundreds of years later, is that the one responsible for giving Francis this experience which resulted in God-realization was in fact the Sufi Spiritual Master, Khwaja Khizr, who traditionally is always available to those who need spiritual guidance. Since Francis was at the end of the spiritual path, and making his final surrender he needed the touch of a Perfect Master, but there was no

Perfect Master in Italy at the time, so Khwaja Khizr appeared for Francis, sent by God. Now, whether the angel was Khizr, or there were both Khizr (unseen) and the angel (seen) by Francis is part of the mystery.

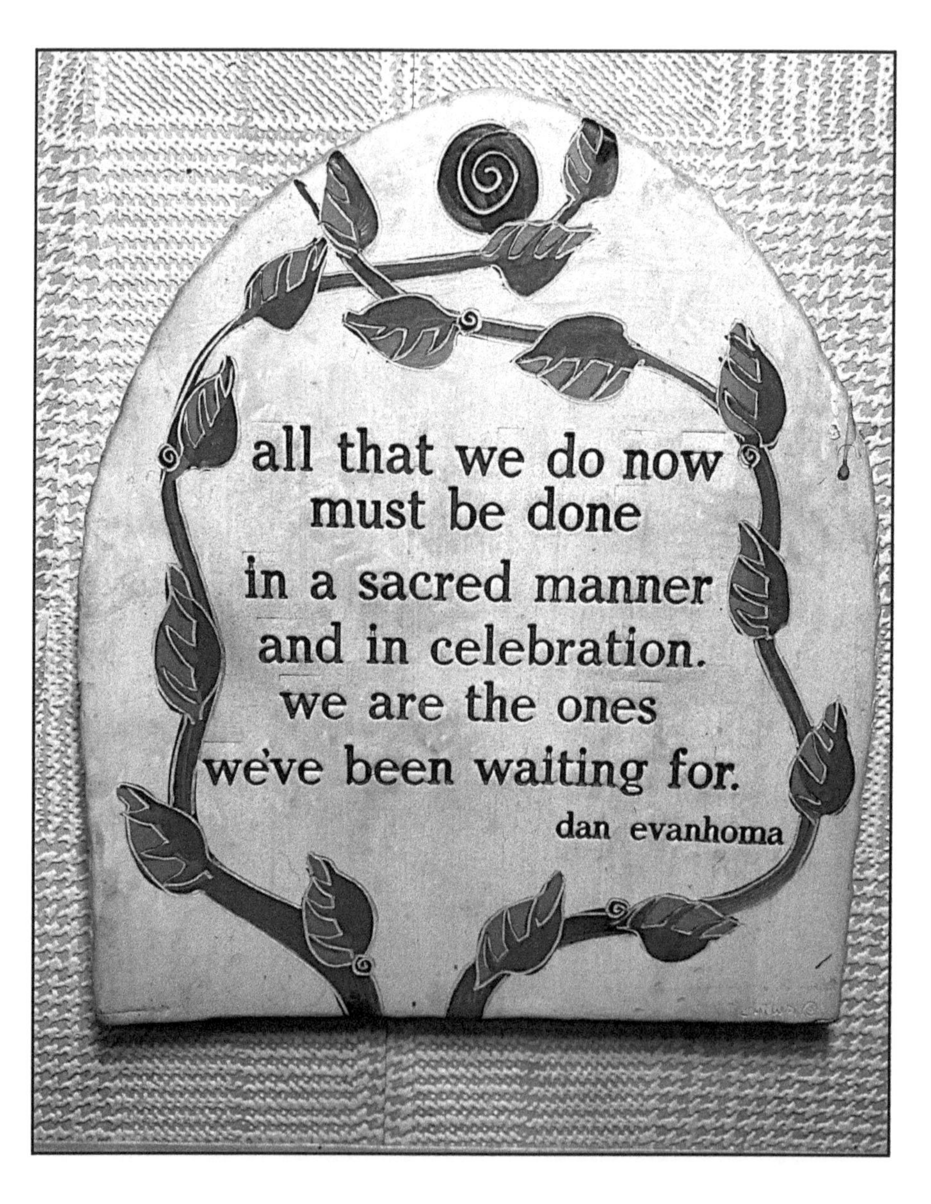

In the 1990s, I had a dream in which I was given an instruction to visit the sacred mountain in Arizona during 1997. I went to the San Francisco Peaks in Flagstaff, Arizona to obey this instruction. From there I visited the Hotevilla Hopi reservation, where I briefly met elder Dan Evenhema. Shortly after he passed away he visited me in spirit at my Flagstaff home with an additional instruction. - L.W.

Chapter Four: The Gift

"In most cases it is only when the aspirant is driven
to realise the futility of all his efforts
that he approaches the Master." [o]
Meher Baba

Someone may ask at this point, but why should I surrender? What is this really all about?

It is multifaceted, but at least in part there is a desire in the disciple to be truly free. Not in the spirit of bargain – "Hey master, I surrender, so unlock my prison cell please!" – but with the knowledge that surrender is the doorway to absolute freedom. Free from the conditions which seem to prevail in the world, such as the neverending lust, anger, greed, violence, and values which lead not to happiness and peace but a continued sense of uneasiness, unhealthy choices, and anxiety. When love is the basis of the relationship with the Spiritual Master of your choice, amazing growth happens. According to Baba the consciousness doesn't need to grow, as a human is a fully conscious being. What needs to shift is the awareness of the inherent divinity within. And what is blocking or obscuring that awareness of your own perfect nature? According to Baba it is mental impressions, or what he calls "sanskaras."

For those who have not heard the word sanskaras before, let's take a moment to define this. A number of Eastern traditions have a similar word, or concept, and the gist of it is simply this. Everything we think, feel, say, and do makes an impression on our mind. The mind is different from the brain, as Meher Baba explained, the mind continues on – after death – along with the soul, and energy, to reincarnate. Then it gets a new body, with a new brain, and the soul and energy and mind use that new form to continue the journey back to the goal, to the Source of Truth. In any case, sanskaras are impressions, and these are the impressions in the mental body. According to Baba, these impressions are vital for the evolution of the consciousness of the soul, and he explained this journey in depth and detail in his seminal book, *God Speaks*. He said these impressions are the veil between the individual and God, and once they are removed the spiritual aspirant will realize God. [1]

Baba himself explains this clearly:

> "... when self-surrender is thorough, the responsibility for your release from sanskaras is devolved upon the Master, and under this new condition the Master annihilates all your sanskaras in no time." [2]

We can see that in and through a loving relationship with the master there is natural transference of responsibility. This is not a mechanical thing, and that is why I keep stressing the foundation of love between the disciple and master. This spiritual process is not a transactional system which requires surrender. This spiritual process is a natural progression from being ignorant of spiritual matters to realizing the importance of love, and then continuing from there to obedience and surrender to a master. When inspired by love, this is the highest experience of relationship I have ever experienced. The Avatars, masters, saints and lovers of God throughout the ages have said the same thing.

There is an old story about an arrogant man who approaches the spiritual master, who is surrounded by a few close disciples, and the man barks at the master, "What does the enlightened one expound that is new and different?!" And the master keeps silent, while the disciple answers for him, "If the master expounded what was new and different he wouldn't be the enlightened one." This is a great example of the nature of the ego, wanting the truth to be something other than what it is, something new and exciting. Of course the experience of the truth is new and exciting for each soul who takes this spiritual journey, but the capital-T Truth has always been one and the same, so say the masters of wisdom.

Baba once explained, "..all that is required for Self-realization is to come into harmony with everything in Creation." He further clarified that this also means coming into harmony with the existence of Spiritual Masters and the Avatar, because these masters are always helping souls spiritually, and to reject this help creates an impediment.

Baba clarifies things for us:

> "In most cases it is only when the aspirant is driven to realise the futility of all his efforts that he approaches the Master. By himself he can make no headway towards the goal which he dimly sights and seeks. The stubborn persistence of the ego exasperates him, and in this clear perception of helplessness he surrenders to the Master as his last and only resort. The self-surrender amounts to an open admission that the aspirant now has given up all hope of tackling the problems of the ego by himself and that he relies solely upon the Master. It is like saying, "I am unable to end the wretched existence of this ego. I therefore look to you to intervene and slay it."

He continues,

> "When a person comes into contact with the Master and recognises him as having the state of egoless perfection, he voluntarily surrenders himself to the Master, because he perceives the ego to be a source of perpetual ignorance, restlessness and conflict and also recognises his own inability to terminate it. But this self-surrender should be carefully distinguished from the inferiority complex, because it is accompanied by awareness that the Master is his ideal and as such has a basic unity with the disciple. Such self-surrender is in no way an expression of loss of confidence. On the contrary it is an expression of confidence in the final overcoming of all obstacles through the help of the Master. The appreciation of the divinity of the

> Master is the manner in which the higher Self of the disciple is expressing its sense of dignity." [3]

Baba reveals to us the futility of the spiritual aspirant trying to tackle the problem of separation from God without surrender. Baba has said elsewhere the spiritual path is like this – A disciple's mouth has to eat their entire body, and then the mouth has to eat itself. How is this even possible? It is not, thus the need to surrender.

Elsewhere Baba indicated that while it is possible to make great progress on one's own, that is a path which is quite long and dangerous, whereas the path of surrender to a Spiritual Master is faster and safer. My friend, Daniel Stone encouraged me to add one fine point here that was explained to us by Baba. While progress can be made up to a point without surrender to a Self-realized Master, it is essential for making the leap, from the sixth plane (of feeling) to the seventh plane of Reality and union with God.

Here is one of my favorite sayings from Baba which sums this up:

> "Through unfathomable ways, I lead you to liberation. Accept My rhythm, come in tune with it without reservations. My rhythm of Truth shall redeem you; It will open your heart, it will give you new love." [4]

Right after sharing those words from Baba, my lovely wife Vanessa called me. She asked what I was doing, and I said I was writing about, "How do we surrender?" And she responded, "So, how do we surrender?" We laughed, and I told her that I would send her this chapter. Then she said, "I think for me, Surrender is more of a conversation with God, and forgiveness is more of a conversation with myself... There's only one person you can surrender to and that's God." I think she is right. She also reminded me that Baba said that the path to God is really a series of surrenders:

> "Progress from one surrender to greater surrender is a progression from a minor conquest to a major one. The more complete forms of surrenderance represent the higher states of consciousness since they secure greater harmony between the aspirant and the Master. Thus the infinite life of the Master can flow through the aspirant in more abundant measure. Spiritual advancement is a succession of one surrender after another until the goal of the final surrenderance of the separate ego-life is completely achieved. The last surrender is the only complete surrenderance. It is the reverse side of the final union in which the aspirant becomes one with the Master. Therefore, in a sense, the most complete surrenderance to the Master is equivalent to the attainment of the Truth, which is the ultimate goal of all spiritual advancement." [5]

This is one of my favorite quotes ever from Baba, and it ties into what He says in his seminal book, *God Speaks*, in which he equates the spiritual path with a series of surrenders, known to the Sufis as Fana (or annihilation). These fanas culminate in the final-fana ("fana-fillah" in Persian) which is the giving up of the sense of separateness, letting go of the limited false ego. This "separate ego-life" is not so easily surrendered, thus the need for the series of smaller surrenders leading up to the final giant surrender which results in Oneness with God, or the unlimited Real Ego, which identifies with - I am God.

The phrase fana-fillah is specific to Sufism, and I asked our dear spiritual sister Azita Namiranian about its meaning in Farsi, since she speaks Dari and Farsi natively. She explained, "You disappear in God... Burn into ash and rise from it ... Become nothing, absolute non-being."

Baba goes even deeper in his explanations in *God Speaks*:

> "The third type of fana-baqa is of the seventh plane of the final involution of consciousness and is the real fana-fillah of the Reality and the real baqa-billah of the Divinity. When the impressioned

> consciousness of individualized life is totally and finally relieved of all impressions of the illusion, and when this unburdened or impressionless individualized Self consciously "passes-away-in" the original, divine absolute vacuum to gain the fana-fillah or the "I am God" state, the goal is finally attained. This is the state of real majzoobiyat." [6]

Rumi, the great poet and (according to Meher Baba, a Perfect Master) says:

> Out beyond ideas of wrongdoing and rightdoing,
> there is a field. I'll meet you there.
> When the soul lies down in that grass,
> the world is too full to talk about.
> Ideas, language, even the phrase each other
> doesn't make any sense. [7]

This is wondrous poetry, but what does it mean? It must mean, at least in part, that the field is Oneness with the Truth. Oneness with all that lives. Oneness with God. With the big "S' Self. The Oversoul. The only One. How else could the "phrase each other" not make sense? It means, when you experience the Truth of Oneness, there is no other. There is no "othering." Othering was a word I had never heard, until I met a professor at Northern Arizona University. Please let me tell you this story:

I was at the playground with my daughter Aspen, in Flagstaff, Arizona. Some of my fondest memories in my life are going to play with Aspen at the playground. She was busy playing, and I was busy watching her run hither and yon, and making sure I caught her as she fell off the equipment, when I noticed another father. He was a Native American, to my observation, and he confirmed this later, as you are about to hear.

We spoke a bit, and he explained that while he is part of the Navajo tribe, they don't call themselves Navajo. That is the label given to them by other tribes. I eagerly asked, "What do you call yourself?" And his response touched my heart. He said, "We call ourselves Dine'. It means, 'The People.' You are also Dine'."

I was floored. I didn't ask for him to include me. I didn't ask what Dine' means. He volunteered, and knowing full well how white I was, he included me in his labeling, in his group, in his tribe. He then went on to explain the problem in the world is that of othering. Making someone, or a group of people, other than ourself. It occurred to me, then and there, that he was in fact walking his own talk as he explained all this to me. He gave me some titles of good books to read, and we ended up parting ways. I never saw him again. [8]

During that time living in Arizona I had many experiences of Dine" as well as Hopi, and Zuni culture. Here is a bit of Hopi wisdom, which is exactly the type of sharing I heard from Grandfather Martin Gashweseoma, Emory Holmes, and other friends at the Hopi reservation, when they allowed me to receive their expressed wisdom, and observe their sacred dance:

A Hopi Elder Speaks

"You have been telling the people that this is the Eleventh Hour, now you must go back and tell the people that this is the Hour.

And there are things to be considered...
Where are you living?
What are you doing?
What are your relationships?
Are you in right relation?
Where is your water?
Know your garden.
It is time to speak your Truth.
Create your community.
Be good to each other.

And do not look outside yourself for the leader."

{Then he clasped his hands together, smiled, and said... }

"This could be a good time!
There is a river flowing now very fast.
It is so great and swift that there are those who will be afraid.
They will try to hold on to the shore.
They will feel they are torn apart and will suffer greatly.
Know the river has its destination.
The elders say we must let go of the shore,
push off into the middle of the river,
keep our eyes open, and our heads above water.
And I say, see who is in there with you and celebrate.
At this time in history, we are to take nothing personally,
Least of all ourselves.
For the moment that we do,
our spiritual growth and journey comes to a halt.
The time for the lone wolf (world) is over.
Gather yourselves!
Banish the word struggle from your attitude and your vocabulary.
All that we do now must be done in a sacred manner and in celebration.
We are the ones we've been waiting for." [9]

Chapter Five: Passive Versus Active Surrender

"Surrender to God is attained in love by free will.
Authentic surrender is a choice devoid of fear.
Love provides the vehicle."
Alexander Adhami

I first had the idea of active versus passive surrender in 2017, spontaneously, during a conversation. My wife Vanessa and I were in a "*Discourses*" meeting at the Meher Spiritual Center. Somehow the issue of surrender was raised, and we had a brief exchange with the entire reading group. A female participant said somewhat dramatically, "I surrender ... I just give up!"

I gently offered my perspective regarding "passive surrender" vs. "active surrender" and how the, "I just give up..." statement sounded a bit passive. I shared that ultimately, what I believe Baba is asking for from us seems more like an active type of surrender. She asked me – "Well, what is that?" I responded that it must have something to do with, "Giving over my self-will, or my wants and desires, in exchange for God's Wish and Will – what He wants for me." And of course I added this is not so easy to accomplish, and there are endless opportunities to actively surrender.

Ultimately, the *Discourses* reading group decided not to continue this conversation, as it was a side topic from the theme of the discourse we were discussing. Later, privately, the participant continued sharing and asked me, "Can we have a whole seminar dedicated to surrender?" This book sprang out of my work on that first surrender seminar, which took place in the Fall of 2017. The results of that seminar were profound. [1]

This brings up a story Baba once told, wherein he explains what is needed for God-realization (or Self-realization). Please allow me to paraphrase. Essentially, he said – what is required in order to realize God, the Divine, as your own being, is that you need to come into perfect harmony with everything in Creation. He said not only is this possible, but that it is the Destiny of all souls to achieve this realization. Just not all at the same point in time. Thus we have saints, Masters, sinners, and various shades of bad and good people all on Earth at the same time.

So, he went on saying that the first soul to realize God had no one before him who had achieved that exalted state of consciousness. In other words, for the very first soul who attempted the realization of the Self as God, there was no one to help. Meaning, no one before had achieved this and could explain or lend a hand. Then, because of the state of that soul, and the conditions in the Creation, that first soul did in fact achieve God-realization, and experienced (without a break) Infinite Knowledge, Infinite Power, and Infinite Bliss. That's great. But it created another challenge, a new challenge.

For all souls coming after, there was now in the Creation, a soul who had achieved Self-realization, and was consciously Divine. So what? Well, Baba had said that one has to come into harmony with everything in the Creation, and now in the Creation was a soul with Self-realization. So for soul number two to strive for Self-realization, there was a need to come into harmony with the fact of a Spiritual Master in the Creation. Now, to come into harmony must mean something spiritual in relation to the existing Master. It does. Soul number two has to be receptive to the spiritual help flowing from the Spiritual Master towards all of creation. This is a type of surrender. Being receptive and willing to be helped is a surrender. It may also involve Obedience, and Love. This help from the Spiritual Master can also be called the grace of the Master.

So the short answer to why surrender seems to be, it is needed. Eventually a limit is reached to how much progress we can make without help. And why would we want to do it all alone? Isn't that a form of ego, maybe even "spiritual ego," if there is such a thing. For my part, I welcome the help of my Beloved Master Meher Baba.

Why Meher Baba asked for Active Surrender

Passive surrender, characterized by an exasperated "I give up!" is about exhaustion, weakness, and maybe just plain burnout. While there is nothing wrong with this, it seems to me what Baba is asking for is when we come from a place of strength, and everything is actually going well, and still we surrender to what we know God wishes for us. Not just "giving up."

This reminds me of a joke. A fellow is driving to a job interview, and he really needs this new job. He has been out of work for too long, and he anticipates that he is a good fit for the role, and feels confident going to the interview. As he approaches the workplace destination, he looks up and down the street, but there is no place for him to park his car. He goes around the block, and still nothing. He looks at the time, and he is running out of time if he is going to be punctual and responsible. At this moment, he calls out to God saying, "If you find me a parking spot, I promise, I will dedicate my life to you, and change my ways, and..." Just then a car pulls out of a parking spot in front of him and he immediately adds, "... never mind I've got it."

In my experience it is natural to experience states of what I call passive surrender. When life is experienced as beating you down, or as having no meaning. That sense of contracting hopelessness and overwhelming depression comes like a tsunami across the beachside village of one's life, it can lead to passive surrender. If you have never had an experience like that, great. Many of us have. The problem with passive surrender is that it rarely leads to spiritual freedom. Animals can be subdued, by other animals or by humans. We see this in dog packs, or with primates, and other groups of animals. The subdued animal lays on its back, or offers its paw, or something. This is a type of passive surrender rooted in animal instincts, for self-preservation, and doesn't mean spiritual surrender. It is the acknowledgement of having been subdued.

If surrender causes one to recoil, and slump, and retract from life, wallowing in self-pity, it is hardly progress. That said, with conscious care, surrender can be shepherded from passive to active surrender. In my experience the difference between passive and active surrender is about quality of life, and the resulting attunement to God within, shifting self-will through self-surrender, towards God's Will. This may be experienced as intuition, inspiration, insight, and more, as Baba has explained in detail:

> "First, you all must understand that just as there are seven planes of consciousness – seven spiritual states – so also are there seven states of understanding. It is always seven. The number seven is the divine number.
>
> The seven understandings are:
>
> 1. Instinct
> 2. Intellect
> 3. Inspiration
> 4. Intuition
> 5. Insight
> 6. Illumination
> 7. Realization
>
> Instinct governs the animal world; intellect, humans; inspiration for those humans whose feelings are developed – like poets and artists. Intuition is for those advanced souls who have conscious visions and understanding true to the point. What you understand by intuition is always true. What you understand by intellect is sometimes true and sometimes not.

Souls on the fourth and fifth planes have insight; their understanding is direct, without thinking with the mind. Illumination means seeing God as He is. The understanding is divine. Realization is understanding oneself as God." [2]

Chapter Six: Healthy, Deficient, and Toxic Surrender

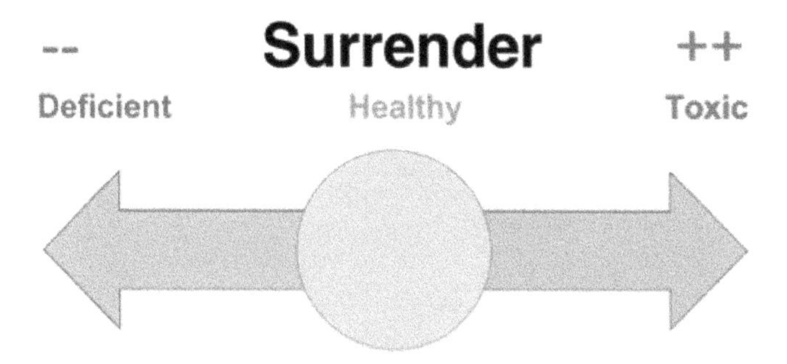

This diagram was created by me for a Forgiveness and Surrender seminar in Myrtle Beach, South Carolina (February 2020).

The purpose of the diagram was to share with the participants my inspiration regarding the message from Meher Baba, "Twelve Ways of Realizing Me." [1]

I was inspired to create a diagram whereby each one of the twelve ways given by Baba would be shown as one of three possible states, sort of like a spinal column, where the middle state is healthy, but it could go "out of alignment" either left or right, by being deficient or toxic respectively. This diagram could be used by a facilitator to help individuals to self-assess their current state around the twelve ways, and how they are manifesting in their life. The healthy state could be described by the facilitator and agreed upon with the participant, and then deficient would be a lack of that, and toxic would be too much in a way that causes harm. Imagine this as a spiritual spinal column.

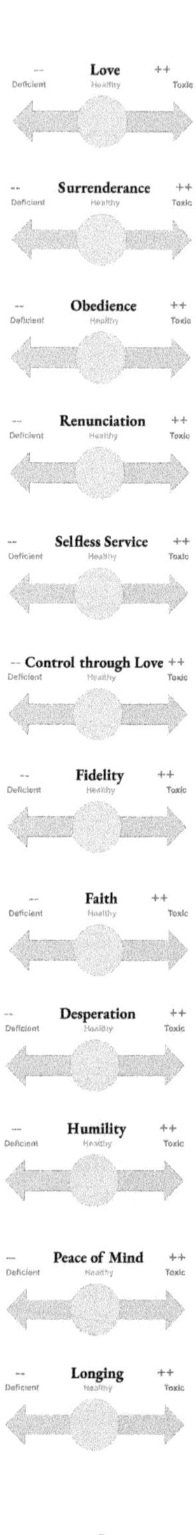
-- Love ++
Deficient Healthy Toxic
-- Surrenderance ++
Deficient Healthy Toxic
-- Obedience ++
Deficient Healthy Toxic
-- Renunciation ++
Deficient Healthy Toxic
-- Selfless Service ++
Deficient Healthy Toxic
-- Control through Love ++
Deficient Healthy Toxic
-- Fidelity ++
Deficient Healthy Toxic
-- Faith ++
Deficient Healthy Toxic
-- Desperation ++
Deficient Healthy Toxic
-- Humility ++
Deficient Healthy Toxic
-- Peace of Mind ++
Deficient Healthy Toxic
-- Longing ++
Deficient Healthy Toxic

Can you self-assess where you are on each of these ways of realizing Baba?

The participants would mark each of the twelve sections with their own feelings, and thoughts, of how that "way" has been working out in their life. For the surrender work we did at the seminar in Myrtle Beach, since we only had two hours set aside for this topic, we had everyone hyper-focused on just surrender. Here is what came from the twenty participants who were invited to write on the diagram:

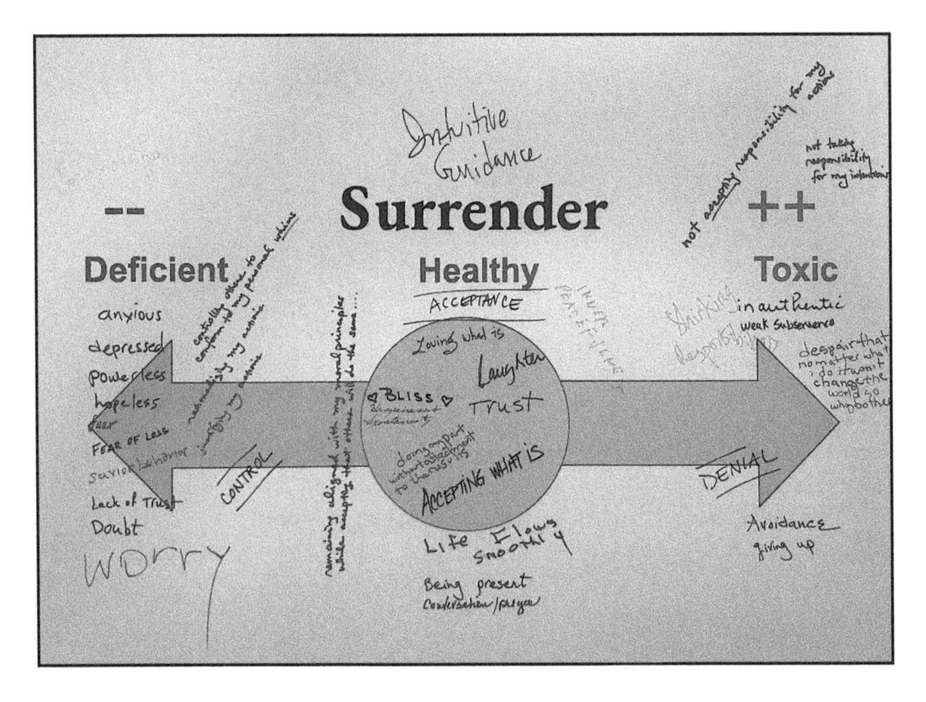

This resulted in three basic categories of participant comments around surrender, or what happens if surrender is deficient or too much in an unhealthy way (toxic). It is important to note that many had difficulty understanding the toxic nature of surrender, but we did get some good results in the end. Here are the results from the first time we tried this exercise with a group:

Healthy Surrender

- Remaining aligned with my moral principles while accepting that others will do the same.
- Conversation/prayer
- Being present
- Remember not to worry
- Accepting what is.
- Doing my part without attachment to the results.
- Trust
- Bliss
- Happiness and spontaneity
- Laughter
- Loving what is
- Acceptance
- Inner peacefulness
- Intuitive Guidance
- Letting Go

Deficient Surrender

- Worry
- Doubt
- Lack of trust
- Survivor behavior
- Fear of loss
- Fear
- Hopeless
- Powerless
- Withholding love
- Depressed
- Anxious
- Controlling
- Control
- Controlling others to conform to my personal whims.
- Rationalizing my actions
- Justifying my actions
- Making up stories

Toxic Surrender

- Giving up
- Avoidance
- Denial
- Exhausting
- Weak subservience
- Inauthentic
- Shirking responsibilities
- Fear-based, "I know best"
- Not taking responsibility for my intentions.
- Not accepting responsibility for my actions.
- Despair that no matter what I do it won't change the world so, Why bother?

The exercise was a great success. From this we can see that there are at least three ways of seeing any surrender, as healthy, or not quite enough, or perhaps too much in a negative sense. My sister, Sarah, reminded me that "one can work on their own perception if there is an awareness of how they are acting out their personal surrenderance." In other words, the purpose of this exercise was simply to raise awareness (individually and collectively) about the nature of surrender, and how we are living that surrenderance in our own lives. I found it helpful, and I received feedback from the twenty participants that most of them found it helpful as well.

Chapter Seven: Evolutionary Resistance to Surrender

While working with Don Stevens, and living in England, I experienced a few insights that came suddenly, like an intuitive flash-of-knowing, quite unexpectedly. I wrote these intuitions in my diary. One of these I titled, "Why we don't surrender," and it is about the reason people are adverse to surrender. Throughout the extremely long process of evolution of consciousness, which according to Baba includes association with countless prehuman forms, such as stones, metals, vegetation, worms, fish, birds, animals, and lastly humans, we experience deeply rooted primal fear. This is a rational fear based on repeated experiences of the food chain and our place in it for ages. This fear can be summed up as – What is trying to eat me? It is accompanied by nearly constant anxiety and a sense of – "looking over one's shoulder," to survive. To not be consumed by another. It is the "Don't eat me," problem.

Once we arrive in the human form, as a result of this long series of evolutionary forms, we are no longer so easily eaten. We hold a spear, or a bow and arrow, or a gun. However there still remains a deeply seated fight or flight response that can be triggered based on this past storehouse of survival impressions. Such psychological triggering can be quite profoundly felt when the human being comes into contact with a Perfect Spiritual Master or the Avatar (Christ), because such a Master can consume the spiritual aspirant – not physically of course – but energetically, mentally, emotionally, and spiritually. In other words, the Master is one of the only beings capable of consuming even the spiritually minded human, and this ancient fear makes it quite difficult for even the spiritual aspirant to completely surrender to the Master.

That's what I saw in a flash.

Speaking of guns, there are two more points that are relevant here to surrender. This may be a little turbulent for some so, "now is a good time to put away your electronic device, and fasten your seatbelt." During Meher Baba's Blue Bus tour, he travelled around India, with many women from both the East and West (11 Eastern, and 9 Western to start). Shortly after I came to Baba, I moved to Myrtle Beach, South Carolina to be near the "Baba community" there. One of the prominent workers in our community was Hermes (Lawrence Reiter). He was editing and publishing the multi-volume biography of Baba, titled *Lord Meher.* I became friends with Hermes (a long story for another time), and I actually worked for him during a period of months. In any case, one day during a conversation, he told me a story which I still remember ; He said something like this -- During the Blue Bus tour of India, when Baba drove around with over twenty women, and two of the men Mandali, he had a loaded gun in the glove compartment. At one point, he told Margaret Craske, that she was in charge of the pistol, and that if anything happened to Baba and men during the journey, and as a result they were in danger of being abused by Indian men, that she should not hesitate to use this gun to defend the women mandali in the bus. Here is the list of the first women on the bus and their ages at the time of departure. [1]

Mehera, 31	Kakubai, 52
Mani, 20	Elizabeth, 42
Naja, 30	Hedi, 45
Khorshed, 28	Helen, 60
Soonamasi, 54	Irene, 22
Walu, 38	Kitty, 47
Mansari, 28	Nadine, 54
Gaimai, 38	Nonny, 63
Manu, 19	Norina, 58
Meheru (Jessawala), 17	Rano, 36

"At four o'clock in the early morning of Thursday, 8 December 1938, Baba left Meherabad Hill in the Blue Bus with the following women of various ages... Elizabeth was the main driver, and Eruch and Kaka were seated next to her in the front seat."

Baba later explained in his book *Discourses*, about the best way to deal with sexual abusers, when he said:

> "Thus, for example, when one's mother's honour is on the point of being violated by a lustful desperado and when one defends her by resorting to violence, he is said to have followed the principles of 'selfless violence.'"

What is the point of this sentence from beloved Baba? It is obvious to me that he is indicating that the most spiritual response to an abuser is to stop them, even if it means resorting to violence. So also, in the case of the women Mandali on board the Blue Bus, he gave Margaret a means of defending the honor of all the women. I met Margaret, on many occasions, in New York and in Myrtle Beach. She was a professional dancer, extraordinarily down to earth, and not a pansy. She was for real. I can totally understand why Baba entrusted her with the gun. Oh, and with this new COVID-19 fiasco in the USA, I also bought my first gun in my life. Not for me, but so that in case ignorance becomes empowered, I can protect my wife and children. I won't surrender to toxic ignorance.

God's Original Question "Who am I?"

For the last few years, since the summer of 2014, I have been blessed with being in relationship with the love of my life, Vanessa. After a number of years of working through many issues both in our relationship, and with those relationships around us in friends and family, we have arrived at some sort of graceful plateau, where there is tremendous creativity, and love, and harmony. Don't get me wrong, I'm not saying everything is perfect, but there is tremendous joy and love, and wondrously great quality of life, at least in my experience. This has allowed us to do our first writing project together, a children's book, based on the purpose of

Creation as explained by Baba in his seminal book *God Speaks*. After completing the writing of that children's book with her, I started in earnest on this book on surrender, and naturally have asked her from time to time her experiences of surrender. I'd like to share some of that here with you now.

Vanessa said,

> "Surrender is a conscious journey, you are given one circumstance after another in which you realize the deep need to surrender to – or let go of – an identification with a place or being. We are on this journey of letting go of one thing or another, because the whole journey is really from – "Who am I?" – to finding the true self.
>
> "Awareness goes hand in hand with surrender, that's why it is so special to be a human being. Because, we as human beings have the capacity to take the opportunity to let go of who we think we are and find out who we really are. I think surrender is a direct function of involution, and as we progress towards God (Baba) we are asked to step from one surrender to a greater surrender, until we have surrendered every inch of our entire being."

Surrender and Harmony with all Life

Baba explained,

> "Man cherishes false belief because he relishes it. Throughout his long life as an individual soul he has clung fondly to the false idea of his separate existence. All his thoughts and emotions and activities have repeatedly assumed and confirmed but one affirmation, viz., the existence of the separate "I." To surrender the false belief that he is the ego-mind is to surrender all that has seemed to constitute his very existence. In surrendering the false belief that he is his physical or subtle body it is necessary to surrender various desires and

> attachments. It is a giving up of something one has had for a long time. In surrendering the false belief that he is his ego-mind, he is called upon to surrender the very core of what he has thought himself to be. To shed this last vestige of falsehood is, therefore, the most difficult thing." [2]

Because of the lineage and legacy of the soul's journey through Creation, first in sub-human forms, and then through reincarnation, the experience of the soul has gotten it firmly attached to the idea of its own separative existence. Indeed, the human condition, and experiences of the world reinforce this constantly when encountering aspects of humanity such as anger, greed, hatred, lust and so many other issues. So, spirituality must in some sense be the undoing of all of this, a reversal of these ideas. It may be oversimplified, but antidotes to these toxic beliefs must be along the lines of love, tolerance, generosity, kindness, tenderness, intimacy, surrender and oneness. If we can start to believe in these antidotes, we can start to practice them. The practice of surrender is what we are talking about here. But in order to practice we need some idea of what it is, and how it looks, or sounds, or feels to be surrendered.

"The majestic Cypress tree will look like a weeping Willow compared to the enthralling presence of my Beloved..." Calligraphy by Majid Roohafza of a complete Hafiz poem which we titled "Farrukh" (Beloved). English translation by Azita Namiranian and Laurent Weichberger.

Chapter Eight: Surrender and Separation

I remember that while I was living in Charlotte, I had a glimpse of the relationship between separation from God and surrender. I was given to understand these two powerful experiences, or spiritual forces, actually as being two sides of the same coin. As Rumi says in his "Song of the Reed":

> "Listen to the reed and the tale it tells, how it sings of separation:
>
> "Ever since they cut me from the reed bed, my wail has caused men and women to weep.
>
> "I want a heart that is torn open with longing so that I might share the pain of this love.
>
> "Whoever has been parted from his source longs to return to that state of union." [1]

Here the great poet and spiritual master, Rumi, is explaining that the reed that has been cut from the reed bed, its original home, and feels separation, it is longing to return to the source, a perfect metaphor for that primal longing to be consciously reunited with our Original Real Divine Nature. So, it is coming into tune with this longing caused by separation that leads eventually to surrender, in that we consciously learn to surrender (usually little by little) into that spiritual relationship with God (or the master), so that we can shed our attachments to the limited false ego, and the many fleeting distractions (eg. lust, anger, greed), and the multifarious temptations, and start returning to what is important and lasting.

Recently my son Cyprus turned thirteen. For the occasion I invited three men I look up to, or resonate with, or wanted to put forth to my son as "men" to model after, and we had a "coming of age" ceremony for him at the Meher Spiritual Center in Myrtle Beach. It went great. One of the men, Thomas Wolfe, wrote to me after that he found a ghazal (poem) from the Persian poet, and spiritual master, Hafiz, which mentions both Cypress and Aspen. These are the names of my children. I asked him for a copy of the poem, so I can translate it, and give it as a gift to my children. While I don't speak Persian (Farsi), I have Persian friends, and it seemed like a worthy project. What I didn't expect is that this would fit so perfectly into this book about surrender. I wanted to call this section, What does surrender sound like? But I found the notes on the chapter I planned on "Separation and Surrender," so here we go. We share below the entire Hafiz poem, titled by us "*Farrukh*" (Beloved), and then we will discuss its relevance to surrender:

> My heart's longing for my Beloved is like his tousled hair.
> Only the curls of his dark mane are so fortunate
> to be near the face of my Beloved.
>
> I wish I was that dark fortunate one, as his constant companion.
> The majestic Cypress tree will look like a weeping Willow
> compared to the enthralling presence of my Beloved.
>
> Oh Saqi, pour us your purest wine,
> my zikr is remembering my Beloved's intoxicating beauty.
> This pain of separation from my beloved has arched my back,
> like the curved eyebrows of my Beloved.
>
> Even the aroma of the best Turkish perfume cannot be compared
> to the bouquet of my Beloved's hair.
> If everybody's heart is longing to be somewhere,
> my heart's yearning is only moving toward my Beloved.
>
> I am the servant of those who are so completely like Hafiz,
> who have become a fortunate slave of my Beloved. [2]

Hafiz starts out describing his beloved's hair, and how fortunate the curls of his hair are to be near to his face. Notice how the narrative voice moves from image to image, but there is only longing expressed, as Hafiz asks for nothing, he just praises his beloved, in many ways, and longs just to be nearer to his beloved. This state of longing and surrender is the final step before union. Meher Baba explains all of this much more clearly. It is good to remember that Hafiz was in fact Baba's favorite poet.

Meher Baba said:

> Love is a gift from God to man.
> Obedience is a gift from Master to man.
> And surrender is a gift from man to Master.
>
> The one who loves desires to do the will of the beloved,
> and seeks union with the beloved.
> Obedience performs the will of the beloved,
> and seeks the pleasure of the beloved.
> Surrender resigns to the will of the beloved, and seeks nothing.
>
> One who loves is the lover of the beloved.
> One who obeys is the beloved of the beloved.
> One who surrenders all - body, mind and all else - has no existence
> other than that of the beloved, who alone exists in him.
> Therefore greater than love is obedience, and greater than obedience
> is surrender. And yet, as words, all three can be summed up in one
> phrase: love divine.
>
> One can find volumes and volumes of prose and poetry about love, but there are very, very few persons who have found love and experienced it. No amount of reading, listening and learning can ever tell you what love is. Regardless of how much I explain love to you, you will understand it less and less if you think you can grasp it through the intellect or imagination.

Hafez describes the bare truth about love when he says,

> *Janab-e ishqra dargah basi bala tar-azaq'ast;*
> *Kasi in astan busad kay jan der astin darad.*
>
> "The majesty of love lies far beyond the reach of intellect;
> Only one who has his life up his sleeve dares kiss the threshold of love."

The difference between love and intellect is something like that between night and day; they exist in relation to one another and yet as two different things. Love is real intelligence capable of realising Truth. Intellect is best suited to know all about duality, which is born of ignorance and is entirely ignorance. When the sun rises, night is transformed into day. Just so, when love manifests, not-knowing (ignorance) is turned into conscious knowing (knowledge).

In spite of the difference between a keenly intelligent person and a very unintelligent person, each is equally capable of experiencing love. The quality which determines one's capacity for love is not one's wit or wisdom, but one's readiness to lay down life itself for the beloved, and yet remain alive. One must, so to speak, slough off body, energy, mind and all else, and become dust under the feet of the beloved. This dust of a lover who cannot remain alive without God - just as an ordinary man cannot live without breath - is then transformed into the beloved. Thus man becomes God. [3]

While working on the Hafiz translations with Azita Namiranian, and my wife Vanessa, I asked Azita to open the *Divan of Hafiz*, and ask him which ghazal we should work on next. Here is what came from that exercise in surrender. I felt it was a perfect answer and it was exactly relevant to all I was struggling with in my life at that moment. Perhaps asking for help from the Divine is itself a type of surrender? Hafiz says:

That King of kings, our beloved is stealing the hearts of His Lovers,
one glance of his beauty enchanting them,
broken hearted and intoxicated with love,
they rush to his side.

He joined my path and approached this dervish with His intoxicating presence, addressing me as "Mashuq," his sweetheart among the inspired poets!

He asked me, "How much longer will you live alone like a poor fakir, when you can live abundantly just as my fortunate slave?"

"If even that tiny speck, like a dervish, spins around the sun – don't sell yourself short!
Love me, and you'll find yourself whirling towards the heart of the sun itself!"

"Don't depend upon anything in this harsh world, instead
pour into your chalice only gentle beauty and tenderness."
That wine bringer, peace be upon him and his family,
admonished me then to stop associating with deceivers!

Beholding the field of succulent red tulips,
I wonder who was so cruel to break their pure hearts?
So many martyrs drenched in blood.

Hafiz answers his own question,
"You and I are not allowed to lift this shroud of secrecy.
Remain focused on His love, and the beauty of His luscious mouth!"

To escape from the antagonist,
just hold tightly to the robe of The Friend.
Become the man of Yezdan,
and be protected from true evil, Ahriman. [4]

Chapter Nine:
Surrender Anecdotes

"You either want what you want or you want what I want.
You can't want both."
Meher Baba

An Arizona Restaurant

Once, during a period where my work had me traveling all over the state of Arizona, I happened to go into a restaurant in a town I had never visited before. You know those types of restaurants where they have antique signs, and painted saws, and chachkas on shelves, and all sorts of curiosities? Like that. So the hostess grabs a menu, and asks me to follow her. We walked through every bit of the place to a table, all the way in the back corner. I started thinking – where is she taking me? – Finally, she motions to the booth and over the table I see a sign with the words,

> "Half my suffering comes from wanting things my way,
> and the other half comes from getting them my way."

As soon as I saw the sign, I laughed internally and said to Baba, okay now I know why you wanted me at this table. I knew instantly Baba wanted me to read these words, as they are in fact a profound clue in this mystery known as the spiritual path. [1]

Miriam's Inherent Surrender

At one point, while living in Portland, Oregon, I was blessed to have a deep conversation with my friend Miriam Rose, M.D. This helped elucidate some of the points about surrender:

"We all start off unfolding from the first cell that is us. Because there is a Divine Underlying blueprint, that's oriented towards God – or the Breath of Life – that is in all of us from the get-go, and all through our lives it is there. As the embryo grows and changes shape, there's no resistance to that underlying plan, there is inherent surrender to the process of life. It's such a fluid process – there are no doubts, no hardness, or holding back – like water into water. There is no self-assertion of, "I want to do it my way." The embryo just flows into form and life." [2]

The Griffin Home

During my work with Don Stevens, at one point he said to me, if you are in Massachusetts you must go to Salem and meet Cynthia and Richard Griffin. Don had never led me astray, so as fate would have it, I was sent to Massachusetts for work, and I called them up. I told them I had to visit them and meet them because Don told me to, and they laughed and knew exactly what I meant, and lovingly welcomed me. It was the first of many such visits at their home, and on one visit with them, I happened to glance over at their refrigerator and observed what appeared to be Mani's handwriting on a note with a magnet sticking it to the fridge. I walked over and sure enough it was Mani's writing, and it read: "Baba said to us: 'You either want what you want or you want what I want. You can't want both.'" [3]

"Avatar Meher Baba" by Vanessa Weichberger

Chapter Ten: Surrender with Meher Baba

"To live fully do we surrender to the present moment?"
Anne Weichberger

Back in 2010 I was working at JP Morgan Chase, by far the largest firm I have ever been privileged to serve. I was quite happy with the work there, and for a time I was the "India Program Manager" in charge of setting up a new office in India for my division, Retirement Plan Services, which was based in Kansas City, Missouri. In any case, I was going back and forth to India for this work, and at one point in April I was in Mumbai and had a small window of time during which I could steal myself away to Meherabad to see Baba. I knew that the Meher Pilgrim Retreat would be closed for Indian summer, as it is just too hot. I also knew that Meherazad would be closed, and no pilgrims allowed, but I decided to go anyway, just to lay my head once more at Baba's feet in his Samadhi – of course it would be worthwhile. I saw on my JP Morgan Chase schedule that there was a meeting in Pune, and I told my colleagues I needed to attend that meeting. After that meeting, I told everyone I needed to take care of something personal, and would be back in about 24 hours. No one argued. The Indian work culture is much different than in America. I got a taxi from Pune to Ahmednagar, and asked him to take me to the best hotel. I got a hotel room, and then immediately took off for Meherabad in a taxi. Upon arriving at Meherabad I told the taxi to leave me there alone, and he rumbled off down the hill.

Beloved Baba's Samadhi was empty, still, quiet. No line in front of the door. No one there except the Tomb Keeper. It was so hot I could barely walk. My muscles had trouble contracting. I spent a few blessed hours alone with Baba in his Tomb. Eventually I got overheated, and my body started to give me signals to go find a cooler location. I left the Samadhi, got my prasad, and walked down the hill towards the place where the rickshaws gather for pilgrims. There was no one anywhere, except a lone Westerner, Will David, coming up the hill on a bicycle. I met him crossing the railroad tracks, he was coming up as I went down. Since that day I joke that he must be one of Baba's Perfect Masters. Arriving at the rickshaw stand I saw no one. No rickshaws, no drivers, no taxis, nothing. Just hot earth. I hadn't accounted for this. My hotel was miles away in Ahmednagar. I knew Baba had frequently walked that distance, so I turned and started walking towards my hotel. With every step I got hotter and I didn't believe I could make it – and then a van pulled up beside me and asked me if I needed a ride. I said I would like that, and how much rupees did he want. He told me the price, and it was about ten times what that ride is worth in India, so I said no and kept walking. He slowly drove next to me as I walked and we haggled down the price, until I agreed and got it.

At the hotel I cranked up the AC, and cooled down. After a few hours, I hatched a plan. I thought, well here I am and Meherazad is definitely closed. But what if, since I have a copy of my OmPoint International magazine with me, I became the mailman to deliver that copy to Meherwan Jessawala as a gift. Surely a mailman is allowed to deliver the mail? I made up my mind to go for it, and got a rickshaw. The sun was starting to set. I made sure the magazine was in a large envelope with "Meherwan Jessawala" written in big letters on the outside. I got in the rickshaw and made sure he knew how to get to Meherazad. Off we went. Soon we were rolling down that access road to the front gate of Baba's divine abode, and then through the gate and into the driveway. I was acutely aware of how quiet it was at Meherazad when it was closed, and how loud our rickshaw sounded, and how even the tires on the gravel seems to amplify our presence. We rolled to a stop and I motioned to the driver to turn off the engine. Soon a watchman came out to meet us. I said, "Hello, Jai Baba, I have a package here for Meherwan Jessawala." The watchman seemed to understand perfectly, and took the package from me. I then dared to say, "Is he here?" He gestured to me to follow him, and walking rapidly we turned the corner to where Meherwan was sitting on the front porch of

Mandali Hall reading a newspaper. He put down his paper, and turned to me, and said, "Is that Laurent? What the heck are you doing here?"

I said, "Yes, Meherwan, Jai Baba, please forgive me..." and I went into an explanation of JP Morgan Chase bank, and how they brought me over to India, and how could I be in India and not come to Meherabad and Meherazad, and etc. Then I said, "And I know you like to read OmPoint so I brought you our latest issue." At that Meherwan started speaking in what sounded like Marathi to the watchman, who then went into high gear and opened up Mandali Hall. The two main doors were open in front of me, but the lights were not switched on. It was totally dark inside, and only the light streaming in from the doors illuminated Baba's chair. Then Meherwan continued, "Go and put your head at Baba's feet, and leave it there."

He pulled out OmPoint and started to read, and I went into Mandali Hall. I won't speak about that experience except to say, it was the best visit to Mandali Hall I have ever had. Time stopped. I don't know how long I was in there. No one was in there with me. No line. No coming - no going. Just Baba. Naturally, eventually, I lifted my head and departed the hall.

After some catching up, and hugs, I got back in my rickshaw and back to my hotel, and back to JP Morgan Chase in Mumbai, and back to Kansas City, and eventually back home. That twenty four hour visit to Meherabad and Meherazad remains one of the best pilgrimages of my life. Meherwan's guidance, "Go put your head at Baba's feet, and leave it there..." back then I didn't know what it all meant, and now, years later, obviously, it means to me: Surrender.

For the remainder of this chapter, I will discuss what Meher Baba said directly about this topic of surrender, with my commentary about each quote. Please know that anything I seem to understand or share as knowing is based entirely on my life with Baba, and what he has given me to see and comprehend. Without his guidance and love, I would know absolutely nothing.

Many of the quotes I have selected are from the book, *Listen, Humanity*, by Meher Baba, edited by Don E. Stevens. Since Don himself told me how this book came to be, I am sure he would want me to share that story with you before we launch into the material. Don's story itself has elements of love, obedience and surrender in it, so let's see what we can find. This book is about what it was like to live with Meher Baba in India, as a Western man, and what Baba said and did on a daily basis. And, for what it is worth, Baba explained that he was extremely pleased with Don as a disciple. Here I relate the story as Don told it to me, how Meher Baba gave him the project which resulted in the book *Listen, Humanity*.

Don's Story

During the month of September 1954, [1] Baba planned a special three week sahavas only for Western Men to attend. Baba sent out invitations and Don was also invited. As fate would have it, Don ended up with a "Urinary Tract Infection" (UTI) and wrote to Baba about this, saying that his doctor recommended that he not travel to India in this condition. Baba wrote back to Don,

"I will make it up to you."

This was such a tender and heartwarming response, under the circumstances. The sahavas took place at Meherabad as planned and became known as the "Three Incredible Weeks with Meher Baba".

The next year, Baba planned another sahavas, this time for only Easterners, however it was segregated by languages. This became known as the "Four Language Groups' sahavas, because Baba invited the Hindi speakers for a week, Gujarati for a week, Telegu for a week, etc. The sahavas covered a four week period and four distinct Indian languages.

Many Western people think of India as a homogenous whole nation, however culturally it is quite diverse in languages, cuisines, ways of worship, clothing, and more. Now, since Don had not been able to attend that Three Incredible Weeks, Baba sent him an invitation to join this Four Language Groups sahavas, and he went. For what it is worth, Don did not speak any of these languages.

Upon arrival, Baba greeted him in the usual fashion, which Don told us consisted in the regular checking up by Baba, when he asked questions such as, "How did you sleep?" and "Have you eaten?" and finally, "Did you have a good bowel movement?" If to the last question Don replied no, that he was in fact somewhat constipated, due to the long travel, Baba would immediately order one of the Mandali to bring an "orange flavored" drink which was of course a laxative, and Don would thereby be relieved. Next on Baba's list for this particular visit was to take Don to a special room at lower Meherabad, which Baba indicated he had built for Don for this visit. Baba also explained to Don that he was one of only two Westerners invited to this Indian sahavas, the other being Francis Brabazon, from Australia. That explained, Baba actually produced a tiny invoice for the cost of the room construction, and expected Don to pay the amount required. We don't know how much it cost, but that was not the point. The meaning of this, from my point of view, is that Baba built a special place for Don, and asked Don to contribute to that cost. All that settled, Don was ready to commence the sahavas with Baba.

As one can only imagine, there were many opportunities to be with Baba, day in and day out, in intimate companionship with the Avatar. There were some talks, some special activities such as a program created by Baba to "wash the feet of the poor." Baba had his disciples round up some of the poorest villagers from the surrounding area, and then Baba would systematically wash their feet, and bow his head down at their clean feet. Once when I went to India, during the 1980s, I climbed the hill adjacent to Baba's Seclusion Hill, and found a Hindu temple at the top. There was a temple keeper, and I was with an Indian woman, a friend of mine, so we could communicate with him. After some back and forth questions, we found out that when he was a young boy, Baba had created a program of washing the feet of the poor and bowing to them, and he was one of them. Baba had washed his feet and bowed to him. Now he was a temple keeper overlooking Meherazad from the next hill.

Needless to say the time flew by, and eventually the day came when Don had to prepare to depart for home in San Francisco. On that day, Don explained to us, he was packing his suitcase in his room, when one of the Mandali came and said, "Don, Baba is calling you." And, as Don reminded us, when Baba called you, you did not so much as add another pair of socks to your suitcase, you stopped everything and went straight to him. Obediently, Don stopped everything and followed him out of the building to a beautiful sight. There underneath a lush tree nearby sat Baba in a chair waiting. Next to Baba was a small wooden side table, and on the table was a pile of papers, and on those papers Baba had placed a sizable rock.

Upon reuniting, Baba immediately began inquiring,

"Don, I understand you are getting ready to go, and I came to say goodbye and ask if you have enjoyed your time here at this sahavas with me?"

Don naturally said how wonderful it was to be with Baba, for so long and in such intimate sahavas and companionship, and that it was just great. This pleased Baba to hear, and he continued, directly and honestly,

"Well as you can see, Don, I have brought these papers here, and these are my messages which have been collected over the years, and which have not yet been published. They are the quality of messages which I have already explained to you, which have my personal attention and have been given by me and gone over by me."

In other words, Baba was keeping silence since 1925, and the words associated with him as author had different qualities, some having more attention from Baba personally, and some less, and these were of the highest quality.

At this point, Baba picked up the pile of papers from the table, holding his hand out towards Don and continued,

"I was thinking that you might take these back with you, and perhaps create something like a small book from them?"

Don replied with some hesitation, "Oh well ,Baba, that sounds like quite a job, and I am sure you have others who are better suited for that work?"

However, Baba continued, "I will help you."

At this point Don agreed, and received the papers from Baba's hand. But that was not the end of the conversation. Baba continued ,

"There is another thing, as that would be quite a small book. You see, during the entire sahavas here, I have had my secretaries taking down, word for word, everything I have said here, and that transcript can be made available to you. What about the possibility of you sharing your own experiences of being here at the sahavas, and you could use that transcript and what I have said, to create another section?"

With this Don became even more interested, as he had always loved creative writing projects, and this was definitely more creative than the first bit Baba had suggested for the book. Still the conversation was not complete. Baba continued:

"You know, Baba deeply values your own perspectives and insights, so what about the possibility of you writing a section just from your own point of view, be free?"

Don liked this idea as well, and he said so. In the space of a few minutes, at the end of the Four Language Groups sahavas, at Lower Meherabad, Baba had arranged this project meeting for producing a new book, by Meher Baba, but also largely by Don Stevens himself, and the whole project, from the first letter, was the Avatar's own idea. Don just agreed.

The story continues that Don took those papers back to the room, and packed them away of course, precious as they were. I am sure they still exist today in the vaults of Sufism Reoriented somewhere. In due course, Don departed Meherabad, and Beloved Baba's divine company. Don left Mumbai en-route to San Francisco, and after settling in, back at home, he took out those papers again. He described his process to us like this,

"I took those papers out and sat on my bed and began to read them. I immediately saw that there were different subjects being covered and so I began to organize each message into distinct piles by broad topics. When I had thereby organized the entire set of papers from Baba, I began to pick up each pile and see what each pile looked like and it was astonishing. The order in which the messages from Baba ended up in the first pile was such that all I would need to do, as an editor, would be to write a sentence or even just a single word, to stitch them together into a chapter in a book. Then I picked up the next pile and it was the same. And then the next, and each and every pile of messages was like that. Then I remembered what Baba had said to me, sitting in the chair underneath the tree at Meherabad, "I will help you." And I knew this was the help Baba had promised."

So, in conclusion, Don explained that the pile of messages handed to Don from Baba became section two of *Listen, Humanity*. The part where Baba said Don should describe his own experiences at the Four Language Groups sahavas and interweave the transcripts of what Baba had said during those times, became section one. And the writing from Don's own perspective and his enduring insights became section three.

One last note on the title of the book, as some may wish to know what that is all about. Don explained it to us like this: He had worked hard with Baba on the book *God Speaks*, as an editor chosen by Baba for this task. Since he had finished working on that for Baba, he playfully wanted to title this next book in direct relation to *God Speaks*. So, if "*God Speaks*," naturally what comes next? Don said he had chosen the title, "*Humanity Listen.*"

However, shortly after this selected title, one of his close friends who had heard about Don's work on this new book said they had a dream, and in the dream the book was alternately titled, "*Listen, Humanity.*" Apparently this dream convinced Don that this should be the book title. The book was published by the same publisher as *God Speaks*, named Dodd & Mead. When Baba read the book he was well pleased with Don's work.

Here are the selected surrender quotes: [2]

Extremely early on in his spiritual work, Baba started to explain about surrender. If we look chronologically through *Lord Meher*, the multi-volume biography of his life, there are dozens of quotes. Keep in mind, that when Baba said most of these statements, He was silent, and using an alphabet board to communicate, and He had not yet revealed publicly that He was the Avatar. Many people in the world thought of him as either a saint, or a Sadguru (Perfect Master). It is helpful to remember that when reading especially the early quote. Here is one of the earliest, from 1926, Meher Baba explained the different routes to the Truth: [3]

> "The foremost and highest object in life is personally serving a Sadguru and complete surrenderance to him. There is nothing like it for one's divine upliftment!

The second is constant meditation on the divine name.

The third is selfless service, and the fourth is the offering of worship [prayer].

Serving a Sadguru and following his orders to the letter in all matters is like taking a course for a master's degree.

The constant repetition of the Almighty's name, done with love, is like studying for a bachelor's degree. Once one attains the bachelor's degree, it does not take much time to attain the master's degree.

Performing selfless service to humanity without the least selfish motive is like obtaining a high school diploma.

And offering prayers, observing rituals and ceremonies – the dry drills of religious injunctions or shariat – is like learning the alphabet."

It is clear that Baba has created a simile regarding schooling and spirituality, as almost everyone can understand that way of explaining things. This bit from Baba would have been communicated at Meherabad to the Mandali and anyone else fortunate enough to hear Baba. As we can guess by now, Baba puts serving the Perfect Master and surrendering to him as the highest aspiration. Everything else follows after, including loving repetition of God's name (or Baba's name), selfless service to all of humanity, like Mother Teresa of Calcutta (now Saint Teresa). [4]

At the bottom of the list is praying, and observing the ceremonial aspects of any religion. It is the kindergarten where one is learning the basics. That is not bad, basics are needed, especially when one wants to advance. But religion is not the goal. Surrender and serving the Master can be seen as a goal or the goal.

Elsewhere Baba has said:

> "The three most important things on the path to God-realization are love, obedience and surrender. There is no possibility of compromise about these three." [5]

Having been around the Meher Baba community since the 1980s, and reading Baba's books and messages, I can easily recall how frequently Baba stressed these three forces of love, obedience and surrender. I say forces, because love is perhaps the most powerful force known to man. From what I have gathered with Baba, one doesn't normally just jump straight into obedience with the Master. Most people, it seems, start with love, and loving the Master. And then, over many years, maybe even lifetimes, the deeper love evolves or transforms into obedience. It is interesting to note that Baba indicated that love is a gift from God to man, and obedience is a gift from Master to man, which makes it sound as if one doesn't just obey the Master out of the blue, but that there is a relationship built with the Master, and the instructions coming from the Master to the disciple, and subsequently the disciple's ability to have this order, and obey it, are truly a gift. Then it seems, lastly comes surrender. In other words, if there is an order to things, and a sequence, and unfolding, on this journey with God and the Master, then it appears that love dawns first, then slowly obedience and finally surrender. Naturally one could write a whole book on obedience, or love, with Baba, yet we are focused here on the surrender part. When Baba says here, "There is no possibility of compromise," I can interpret that to mean that they are a must-have with Baba. This is like the traditional spiritual song we used to sing, "So High":

> My God is so high, you can't get over Him,
> He's so low, you can't get under Him,
> He's so wide, you can't get around Him –
> You got to come in through the Door (the Lamb).

Don Stevens and Darwin Shaw said that Baba meant it, and Buddha and Baba told it to many people, all in their own ways, they said we have to make the right effort, that we have to strive, we have to do our best, and then allow the Master to help us. One of Baba's most famous quotes is, "Do your best. Then don't worry, be happy in my love. I will help you." Surrender is then at least in part, being open and receptive to the help flowing from the Master. Remember Baba said that while love and obedience are gifts to man from God and the Master respectively, the gift of surrender is from man to Master. When we talk about efforts to overcome the grip of the ego, I am certain now that surrender is one of the most important ways in which we strive to do that spiritual work. That becomes our part of the equation. Surrender = Obedience - Ego / Love (or something).

> Baba said, "When God becomes man (Avatar, Buddha, Christ, Rasool), He can bestow both love and obedience upon and accept the surrenderance of any and all individuals." [6]

Here is a gentle reminder from Baba that when the Avatar comes on Earth, while he is here he gives his love and the gift of obedience to many, and for those who are prepared to surrender he fully receives that offering from them. From the point of view of spiritual history, we can see countless examples of this in the advents of the Avatar, in stories told by disciples of how He behaved while on Earth. It is my personal belief and experience that since Baba is not limited by his form, this work continues even now, and that this is a part of what He called his Manifestation.

> "When man realizes at last that his helplessness is the product of his countless cravings, he tries to find peace by renouncing those cravings and accepting life in a spirit of resignation to the divine will. Until that moment of supreme self-determination occurs, however, he finds himself persistently haunted by an overpowering desire to perpetuate his self-created ego-life. Although he tries desperately to break through the self-centered isolation that this life fosters, it is

> only when he surrenders to a Perfect Master that he is initiated sooner or later into the path of redemptive love. Surrender to the will of the master is in itself very difficult but it becomes more so under the gaze of friendly onlookers. To them the actions of the spiritual aspirant often seem incomprehensible, as if he were sacrificing his most precious possession–his free will. Often it seems to the onlooker that the master aims only to increase his own prestige by directing the actions of those who surround him. This falls far short of understanding the work of the master." [7]

Here Baba is discussing how difficult it is to overcome the forces of the ego, which elsewhere he likens to a hydra-headed dragon. No sooner have you succeeded in killing off one part, but another part rises up again. This is made more difficult when one is surrounded by unsupportive people in one's life. I believe this is why the Buddhists place so much importance on the three pillars of Buddha, Dharma, and Sangha. Naturally, Buddha is the Master, like we have our Meher Baba. Dharma is tricky to translate but it is the wisdom tradition itself, the teaching, the way. And the Sangha is the community. In the same way, it is extremely helpful to surround oneself with one's spiritual community who can be supportive during this tender time of surrender to the Master. Our community does understand, to some extent, the work of the Master. We have a great opportunity to be that support system for each other, one day at a time, if we can see it and experience it as such. In what ways can we help each other to surrender more and more to Avatar Meher Baba, or one's personal master?

> "... it is necessary for the soul of the seeker to be bathed through self-surrenderance in the light that the master affords." [8]

This is one of those rare quotes from Baba that is easily overlooked, but it is oh so powerful to behold. Here he is saying that the soul of the aspiring disciple needs to be bathed in light from the Master, based on this act of self-surrender. Wow. I want to be bathed in Baba's light! And how? By surrendering more and more to him, he gives me, his child, a bath in his light of love. The word "bathed," implies purification, and cleansing, and freshness. This is sounding like a great journey back to Oneness after all.

> "When a man determines to find peace and fulfillment through the renunciation of the cravings of the ego-life, he finds that his new decision is challenged more by the deep-rooted compulsions of his own mind than by any obstructive factors in the external environment. Although he now longs to love the master whole-heartedly as the divine beloved, and tries to surrender completely to him, he is far from being master of his own mind. He cannot even surrender the things he regards as his own, despite his sincere decision. ... But with the first surrender to the master the death knell of the ego-life is sounded, and though it continues to struggle for survival its days of dominance are numbered." [9]

Now Baba is helping us to understand that this is not a one-and-done type of path with surrender. He is encouraging us, and teaching us, that the ego won't give up so easily, and even what one thought may be trivial to let go could be difficult. As Baba said, the ego blocks the flow with attachments to "I, my, me, and mine." Here we are again, getting real with Baba about what to expect on this path. Yet the encouraging news here is, we are not alone, it is not effort in a vacuum but with Baba's help and grace. Once we are determined, or as Eruch said we become, "Determined to be His," then it all comes together eventually, in the result our hearts yearn for, in reunion with him.

> "The false, separative ego tries its utmost to postpone its own dissolution by resisting the divine love of the master. It struggles in the quagmire of existence, but each act of ego-affirmation invites a reaction of deep surrender to the beloved's will. This in turn brings with it the clearer realization of the master as being none other than the irresistible truth that is the Self of all selves, and the one reality in the apparent multiplicity of individual souls." [10]

Here Baba continues explaining the game, the give and take, and back and forth of it all. The ego's resistance to love. The push and the pull of ego assertion and then back to surrendering to our Beloved Master. The perception of the goal, and then the feeling again of being stuck, surrounded by Maya, and the darkness of this gross world. Eventually it is the surrender, according to Baba, which brings us back to the deepest realization of reality.

> "Truth-realization is born of such complete surrender to the engulfing love of God, of which the master is the physical symbol and the channel." [11]

I love when Baba speaks this way, as the Master being a symbol of God's love, and also the way through which God's love flows into the world. This is exactly how I experience Baba. In fact, before meeting Baba (in my heart) I had a lot of difficulty grasping God, God's love, and the purpose of religion. Upon embracing Baba as my Master, I feel and experience God's love flowing to me from him. Baba made this all real to me, instead of some ancient or distant divine mystery. I have had dreams of Baba, showering me with love and his presence. I have heard him talk to me in my dreams, and even a few times I have heard his voice clearly speak to me. I would like to share one such story here now.

It was in the early 1990s and I had recently moved to Myrtle Beach. I was visiting the Meher Spiritual Center, and the most special place there for me is the Lagoon Cabin, where Baba used to sit and receive his followers and anyone who was interested to meet him privately. It is a small square cabin, about twelve feet by twelve feet, with two doors, one facing the ocean, and the other on the next wall, facing the heart of the center. People used to line up at one door to see Baba, who sat in a chair. They would enter, and see Baba sitting right in front of them, and then when their visit was over, they would turn to the left, and exit out the other door. This kept a flow of people moving through the cabin.

In any case, we go there frequently now to spend time alone with Baba. His chair is there, and to me his presence is there strongly. This particular day I was struggling with a long distance romantic relationship, with a woman living on an island in the Caribbean, hundreds of miles away. It was an impossible situation and I was at my wit's end. As I sometimes did with Baba, if the Lagoon Cabin was empty, and I wanted to be most natural with him, I would speak to him out loud as if He was in his chair. To me he is still here with us, so I would treat him that way, like I would speak if he was sitting there in the 1950s.

So, I entered and turned to Baba in his chair and said,

"You see Baba, the reason I am afraid to love..." and I was about to explain the details of my struggle with this long distance relationship when Baba suddenly and rather loudly cut me off in mid-sentence, saying,

"Never be afraid to love!"

That was it. I heard it loudly and clearly, and it spun me around and I immediately went out the door I had come in. I put my shoes on, and in a bit of a love-daze stumbled down the path towards the Original Kitchen. At that time, there were no mobile phones, and there was only one phone at the Baba center for us to use, on a table in a nook, in the kitchen.

There I was stumbling down the path and from the open door of the kitchen comes a voice, saying, "Laurent, the phone is for you. You have a call." I was amazed at this news, but couldn't imagine who would be calling me at the Baba center. As Baba would have it, it was Vanessa, the woman I had been trying to complain about to Baba, calling me from Cayman island in the Caribbean. Over twenty years later, and after much love water under the bridge, we got married. The timing of that phone call was truly remarkable, and I can still hear Baba's voice in my heart saying, "Never be afraid to love."

Let's return to what Baba shares about surrender and its relationship with separation. He said, "The strength, in fact the very being, of separative existence is derived from identification of the self with one of two opposites. This results automatically in distinction from the other opposite. Real merging of the limited self can only be achieved in the ocean of universal life. This involves the surrender of all sense of contra-distinction in form, belief, or action, the surrender of all separative existence in all categories." [12]

Here Baba is giving us a how-to lesson in surrender. It is in fact a type of definition of surrender as the letting go of the sense of separateness from others. I personally struggle quite a bit with this, as my ego likes to latch on to the sense that I am better-than, or know-better, in the way I believe or behave, so this hits home for me. I notice Baba also mentions, "form" as well. I need to be more mindful of how I create separateness based on the forms of things. My goodness, How does one overcome all these types of separative thinking? Apparently through love, acceptance, tolerance, forgiveness, and extremely mindfully.

> "In fact, increasing surrender to the guidance of the master involves drastic curtailment of deceptive imagination–the roots of which are deeply imbedded in the mental and emotional past of the pilgrim. With the gradual transmutation of the aspirant's imaginative faculty into divine consciousness, the veil of ignorance becomes steadily less opaque. In the end, all imagination comes to a standstill and is replaced by the true everlasting realization of God as the sole reality. Thus "the journey," like everything else in duality, is also an imaginative one, but it leads ultimately to final and enduring knowledge unclouded by any kind of imagination or transitory fantasy." [13]

Here Baba is refocusing our attention on the reality of God alone being real, and Oneness as the true nature of things. Perhaps he is hinting at the fact that the more one can see that God alone is real, the less force the ego can exert on the conscious mind? Perhaps these truths, and remembering the truth of Oneness is able to dispel the darkness and the illusions of separateness? It is fascinating that Baba talks about the imagination being linked to the emotions of the spiritual aspirant.

The way he speaks, it sure sounds as if mental and emotional baggage is a large part of the veil of ignorance. It is as if believing in the emotional turmoil is part of the problem, and that our transformation from mental and emotional life to a more spiritual life built on the foundation of God as the sole reality, is the antidote to such a toxic past. Whew. I can relate deeply to this one, as my own past, as far as I can remember in this lifetime, has quite a lot of emotional turmoil moving through it since I was a child. I am sure many people can relate to that.

It would seem part of my effort, or striving, to overcome this deep rooted and deceptive imagining based on emotions is to become more detached from my own past. This means to me, to have compassion for what I have come from, what I have endured on this path, but rather than dwelling on that, to dwell in the present moment more and more with Baba, in this new attitude of God alone is real, and my surrender to him is much more important than my past. This is my striving now.

> "The easiest and safest way to lose one's finite ego is by surrendering completely to the Perfect Master or to the God-man (Avatar), who is consciously one with truth. In them the past, present and future of the individual are drowned and during his implicit obedience to the master he is no longer bound by those actions, good or bad. Such complete surrenderance is in itself complete freedom. Of all the high roads which take the pilgrim directly to his divine destination, the quickest lies through the God-man (Christ, Messiah, Avatar). In the God-man, God reveals Himself in all his glory, with his infinite power, unfathomable knowledge, inexpressible bliss and eternal existence. The path through the God-man is available to all those who approach Him in complete surrenderance and unwavering faith." [14]

In my estimation, Baba is summing up the path with him right here. As I believe Baba was and is consciously one with the truth, I have been surrendering to him more and more. I love that he says, "the past, present, and future" become drowned. This reminds me of his previous quote where he says that the veil of ignorance is related to the past emotional state of the disciple. I look forward to my past being drowned in him, and my becoming free. This reminds me of the conversation Eruch once had about "free-will" and if we have it or not? Eruch's poetic and masterful answer was something like – "I have exercised my freedom to become His slave."

Since we seem to have free-will, and seem to be able to make an effort, what is there "for us to do" on this spiritual path? If we take Eruch's example, we can exercise our freedom, and free will, to surrender to him and become his slave. According to both Baba and Eruch, this leads to real freedom, paradoxically. Baba said, "...complete surrenderance is in itself complete freedom." How can the ego-mind make sense of any of this? It cannot, because it is not logical or rational. It is a heart journey, a love offering of self back to Self. How can we speak of these things? I cannot, but Baba can, as the receiver of surrender:

> "Although God is more easily accessible to ordinary man through the God-men, yet God also reveals himself through His impersonal aspect, which is beyond name, form, and time. Regardless of whether it is to be through His personal or His impersonal aspect, it is necessary that the aspirant seek Him and surrender to Him in love." [15]

> "Complete surrenderance to the God-man is not possible for one and all. When this is not possible, the other high roads which can eventually win the grace of God are:

1. Loving obedience to and remembrance of the God-man to the best of one's ability;

2. Love for God and intense longing to see Him and be united with Him;

3. Being in constant company with the saints and lovers of God and rendering them whole-hearted service;

4. Avoiding lust, greed, anger, hatred, and the temptations of power, fame, and faultfinding;

5. Leaving everyone and everything in complete external renunciation and, in solitude, devoting oneself to fasting, prayer and meditation;

6. Carrying on all worldly duties with a pure heart and clean mind and with equal acceptance of success or failure, while remaining detached in the midst of intense activity; and

7. Selfless service of humanity, without thought of gain or reward." [16]

Reading this message about the Highroads, was perhaps one of the earliest turning points in my relationship with Beloved Baba. I first encountered it shortly after I came to Baba in the late 1980s. When I read it I had only been with Baba a short time, and certainly as a twenty-something new Baba-lover didn't feel I knew anything at all about surrender. After reading that first sentence, "Complete surrenderance to the God-man is not possible for one and all..." I was sure Baba meant me, so I read with interest these highroads, and felt most drawn to this one: "Being in constant company with the saints and lovers of God and rendering them whole-hearted service." I said to myself – Well, I can do that. My first spiritual experiment, or deep effort, in relation to this was an offer to my dear friend Lyn Ott, who was blind at that time, that I would accompany him and assist in his journey to Meherabad, India. [17]

I felt Lyn was a lover of God (certainly he loved Baba), and was perhaps a saint. Who am I to know? I believed I could be of service to him, and so off we went. I was extremely naive and inexperienced, however I did my best. As Baba would have it, it was one of the most difficult trips of my life, because Lyn became gravely ill, and had to be hospitalized three times in India, once in Ahmednagar (a small local hospital), again in Pune (much nicer), and finally in the best hospital we could find in Mumbai. I learned so much about Lyn, myself, and Baba during that trip, and it was also the trip on which I met my future wife, Vanessa. In any case, I can highly recommend the high roads, to anyone serious about making an effort, and this particular one holds ample opportunities for service in my experience. It is important to note that rendering of whole-hearted service, if done sincerely, is a type of surrender. It is a self-denial in favor of the needs and concerns of another, without fuss or seeking acknowledgment or praise. It is a surrender which seeks absolutely nothing in return.

> "The only way to live a life of absolute inaction is to surrender completely to a Perfect Master. Then one dies entirely to oneself and lives only for the Perfect Master, acting and fulfilling the dictates of the beloved one." [18]

This message from Baba is an extension of what I was trying to say about service being a surrender. It is like starving the ego, because instead of chasing ego driven desires, one is tuning in more and more to the needs and wishes of the Lord. One may think this can only be done with a living Master, however Baba made it crystal clear that this is now the age of intuition, and the connection to him internally. He said in his Last Message on the Alphabet Board that the inner link to him is what is most important and that the external link to his form was only needed in order to establish the inner link. Now that we have him, we can continue this relationship internally. This is the spiritual life, and the path is within.

> "Besides keeping God before us in our daily lives and loving Him by loving our fellow men, we can love God by surrendering to the Sadguru or Perfect Master who is God's personal manifestation, or to the God-man, who is God descended directly into form. To surrender to any of these is to surrender to God Himself." [19]

This seems to be a validation of the importance of the surrender to the Master as a representative of God on Earth. When one has the relationship to the Self-realized Master, or the Avatar, there is the manifestation of God in human form to surrender to, and that is equivalent to surrender to God.

> "To love me as I love you, you must receive my grace.
> Only my grace can bestow the gift of divine love.
> To receive my grace you must obey me wholeheartedly
> With a firm foundation of unshakeable faith in me.
> And you can only obey me spontaneously as I want
> When you completely surrender yourselves to me
> So that my wish becomes your law
> And my love sustains your being.
> Age after age, many aspire for such a surrender
> But only very few
> Really attempt to surrender to me
> Completely as I want.
> He who succeeds ultimately
> Not only finds me
> But becomes me
> And realizes the aim of life." [20]

> "Like a tree, such love has branches—branches of wholehearted devotion, perfect selfless service, self-denial, self-sacrifice, self-renunciation, self-annihilation, and truth. In this love are embodied

> all the yogas known to saint and seeker. The highest aspect of this love, which surpasses love itself, is that of complete surrender to the will of the Beloved. This means complete obedience to His wishes regardless of the cost." [21]

Now Baba seems to be defining the spiritual path for those who may still be confused about what this all means spiritually. He leaves little to the imagination here, when he details this careful list of qualities the disciple must inculcate on the path back to him. Love and devotion, self-denial and service, renunciation and sacrifice, self-annihilation and the truth itself. Doesn't sound easy, does it. Who wants to sign up for self-annihilation? Maybe that's why Baba said it is not possible for everyone to accomplish this right now. However, we can make efforts, we can strive, and He is patience and compassion personified. He understands what we can and cannot do. He knows.

> "When one truly loves God, that love is based on the desire to give up one's whole being to the Beloved. When one loves a Perfect Master, one longs to serve him, to surrender to his will, to obey him wholeheartedly. Thus pure, real love longs to give and does not ask for anything in return." [22]

Here we are again, with Baba and the how-to instructions, about how to surrender, and what not to do. Give but don't ask. Love, which leads to obedience and surrender. It's all sounding simple, it is just found to be more difficult in practice. Few are even attempting this, as most are still out there caught up in the emotional swirl and the fulfillment of desires, seeking gratification and pleasure. However, the life of chasing ego desires seems always to end is some type of suffering, instead of lasting happiness.

> "... those very few who have cast off the veil of duality experience the soul itself without confusing it with any medium or vehicle, and in this experience the soul consciously knows itself to be identical with

God. In the realization of the truth of this oneness, life finds freedom from all limitation and suffering, for it is the self affirmation of the Infinite as infinity. In this state of spiritual perfection the ego-life has been finally and completely surrendered in the experiencing of divine truth. God is known and affirmed as the only reality." [23]

* * *

During the extraordinarily hot summer months in India, Baba would relocate to a villa known as Guruprasad in Pune. This was a little cooler than his normal headquarters at Meherazad, near Ahmednagar. During this time he would allow some visitors to Guruprasad. On one occasion during 1953, a woman was brought to him as she had been suffering from mental illness, and someone asked Baba to heal her mental condition. Baba gave the woman his blessing. [24]

Apparently this served as a catalyst for an extremely important message to come from Baba titled, "The Highest of the High." The next three surrender quotes from Beloved Baba are a part of his much longer message, which we will not reproduce here, but only excerpt the parts directly about surrender:

"They cannot obligate me who surrender their all–body, mind, possessions–with a motive. Nor can I be snared by those who surrender because they understand that to gain the everlasting treasure of bliss they must relinquish passing possessions. A desire for greater gain still clings to their surrenderance, and therefore the surrender cannot be complete." [25]

"I am not to be attained by those who, through love of me, stand reverentially by in rapt admiration. I am also not for those who ridicule me and point at me with contempt. Nor am I here to have tens of millions flock around me. I am for the select few who, scattered among the crowd, silently surrender to me their all – body,

> mind and possessions. Still more, I am here for those who, having surrendered all, never give another thought to their surrender. All those are mine who are prepared to renounce even the very thought of their renunciation and who, keeping constant vigil in the midst of intense activity, await their turn to lay down their lives for the cause of truth at a glance from me. Those who have indomitable courage to face cheerfully the worst calamities, who have unshakable faith in me and are eager to fulfill my slightest wish at the cost of happiness and comfort, these indeed truly love me." [26]

> "Seek me not to extricate yourself from predicaments, but find me in order to surrender yourself wholeheartedly to my will. Do not cling to me for worldly happiness and short-lived comforts, but adhere to me through thick and thin, sacrificing your own happiness and comforts at my feet. Let my happiness be your cheer and my comforts your rest." [27]

This is where Baba seems to further define what surrender means, and it seems to be linked to self-effacement or the denial of what the ego is seeking in favor of pleasing the Lord. If the Lord is comfortable, that allows me to rest. If the Lord is happy, then only can I be happy also, otherwise, what is the point of my existence? From the purely psychological point of view, modern psychology would call this a toxic codependent relationship with a master who is manipulative. But this book is not about "Psychology with Meher Baba," it is about the unraveling of the ego at the hands of the Beloved. If psychology is more important than spirituality, this book, and this surrender path may not be right for you.

Speaking of psychology, there is one more point I am reminded to add here and that has to do with surrender and triggers. "A trauma trigger is a psychological stimulus that prompts recall of a previous traumatic experience. The stimulus itself need not be frightening or traumatic and may be only indirectly or superficially reminiscent of an earlier traumatic incident..." [28] I have been dealing with triggers consciously in myself, and in close relationships, for a number of years. A whole book could be written on surrender and triggers, however I just wanted to make a few points quickly here.

When dealing with triggers in myself, it is quite difficult for me to feel connected, peaceful, loving, compassionate and kind. We recently watched a video of "Thich Nhat Hanh," the famous Buddhist monk, being interviewed by Oprah Winfrey. [29] He gave some wise advice about how to behave when triggered. One of the things he said was to remain in relationship with the one who "caused" the trigger, and try to speak up, saying, "I am suffering. I am trying to practice. Please help me." This of course is in contrast to withdrawing. My wife, Vanessa, says when I am triggered I become a turtle, and withdraw into my shell, and she doesn't like that. So I have started trying to say that phrase he gave us, and it helps me to remain connected when I want to just walk away and be alone. Another point is that just because someone is triggered and upset, and making demands from that place, doesn't mean this should be taken seriously as a request or demand. If it is coming from that primal, lizard-brain, which easily embraces the flight/fight/freeze responses to a psychological trigger, and can manifest as quite illogical and even present as crazy, when compared to a "normal," peaceful functioning adult. [30]

I believe it is important to allow each person to have the dignity of their own process, their own triggers, without rushing in to make them feel better. This spiritual path never was, is not and never will be about making the spiritual aspirant feel good. There are many places to go to feel good, you can go to the beach and play in the waves, or do a wine tasting at a vineyard at sunset. This path ends with bliss, according to Baba, but until then it can be excruciating, as we are asked to let go of everything.

While Don Stevens was with Baba during the Four Language Groups sahavas in India, Baba had posted some messages and circulars on the walls for the spiritual seekers, and Baba-lovers and disciples to read. I quote from these because to me they give a real sense of the atmosphere and spirit around Baba, while he allowed people into his intimate sahavas, which he described as a, "give and take of love."

> "I want you to read carefully and absorb these directions... No one, and that also includes those who have come for the sahavas, should under any circumstances – either directly or indirectly–ask me for favours, rewards, money, jobs, health or other material things, not even for spiritual gain. The best is not to ask for anything. If anything at all is to be asked for, then first one should ponder whether one has the required degree of determination and courage to ask for the love of Baba. If one has that much determination and courage, one should be ready to surrender so completely as literally to give up and let go of everything – body, mind and heart. And the self should be able to remain alive and dead simultaneously." [31]
>
> "For spontaneous surrender the heart must, so to speak, be worn on one's sleeve. One must be ever ready to place one's neck under the ever-sharp knife of command of the beloved, and the head should figuratively be detached in order that it might be completely surrendered at the master's feet. Obedience should be so complete that one's concern with it makes one as much awake to possibilities as it makes one deaf to impossibilities – as envisaged by the poet:
>
> > *"Darmiyane qahre darya*
> > *Takhta bandam karda-ee*
> > *Baad mi gu-ee kay*
> > *Daaman ter makun hoshyar baash."*
> >
> > "I was tied to a raft and thrown in the ocean and then I was warned to be careful not to let my robe get wet." [32]

At this point Baba is making it rather clear that *this spontaneous and complete surrender to the Master is almost impossible to achieve.* What else could be the meaning of being thrown into the ocean tied to a raft and making sure to not get wet. So what's the use in trying? Am I just crazy to follow Baba this way? It is the impossibility of the task, the sense of knowing that of my own I cannot do it, but with the Master's Grace all things are possible which encourages me to keep going. If Baba said to me – "Sorry, you have to do this alone, I can't help you." I am not sure what I would do. But I can assure you it wouldn't be the same. It is because of his constant encouragement, love and guidance that I keep on keeping on. I am in this for the long haul and I haven't given up yet. I feel more detached, and more perspective on my emotions. Naturally, I still get triggered, and upset, but the grip is not as tight. I go longer between feeling overwhelmed by the ego forces, and I continue to feel encouraged by the light of Baba's Love and Grace.

Chapter Eleven: Surrender in Song

There are two songs which in my mind are the closest to expressing surrender that I can imagine, and which I will share below. The first is quite old, and it is one I used to sing when I first came to Baba. It's actually a hymn, and I had heard that Baba loved it, and said it is the Bhagavad-Gita in a nutshell. This is the hymn, "Take my Life, and Let it be." [1]

Take my life, and let it be
Consecrated, Lord, to Thee;
Take my moments and my days,
Let them flow in ceaseless praise.

Take my hands, and let them move
At the impulse of Thy love;
Take my feet and let them be
Swift and beautiful for Thee.

Take my voice, and let me sing
Always, only, for my King;
Take my lips, and let them be
Filled with messages from Thee.
Take my silver and my gold;
Not a mite would I withhold;
Take my intellect, and use
Every power as Thou shalt choose.

Take my will, and make it Thine;
It shall be no longer mine.
Take my heart; it is Thine own;
It shall be Thy royal throne.

Take my love; my Lord, I pour
At Thy feet its treasure-store.
Take myself, and I will be
Ever, only, all for Thee.

Another song that fills my heart with yearning, sadness and that longing for Baba that is ineffable, is the seminal Buz Connor composition, "Surrender." I present Buz's lyrics here, for even without the melody they are amazing to behold. I know Buz a little, and from what I know he is a true mystic, and I honor his profound relationship with our Lord Meher: [2]

This world is filled with fire and fury, storms of ages roar,
But there's a mystery behind the story the heart cannot ignore.
My world's been broken by you, and I've gone under.
What else can I do? Oh, surrender.
There was once a field of my own planting, ready to be reaped,
But now that garden so enchanting has become ashes at your feet.
Should I be running from you, I have no answers.
What else can I do? Oh, surrender.
I must do my best to lay it down, and let my Father take over.
If the hopes and schemes of my imagination had all come true,
Would I be even one step closer to the sight of you?
You tear down the false around you, so truth can be heard.
What else can I do? Oh, surrender.
I must do my best to lay it down, and let my Father take over.
And He comes to turn the heat up higher,
though the journey may be far.
We have the chance to dance in the fire of the Avatar.
You take the pain of the world upon you, for just one word.
What else can we do? Oh, surrender.
I must do my best to lay it down, and let my Father take over.
You take the pain of the world upon you, for just one word.
What else can we do? Oh, surrender

Chapter Twelve: Surrender and Wellbeing

"Just offer your self-will over to a higher-power for guidance, and smile and wave."
Bill Miller

During March of 2020, the situation in America, and around the world, has started to get rather frantic. As I write these lines, the world is convulsing from the effects of COVID-19, a virus which has been spreading rapidly and causing fear and sometimes panic. We met as a Meher Baba community, on-line in a "Zoom" meeting, led by Annie Fahy to discuss how we are coping, and what we do to remain centered with Meher Baba. It was great to meet with my "sangha," as the Buddhist's call the community, and share our strengths and weaknesses, and our connection to Baba, or how we get back to it when we start to waiver. [1]

There is a lot of fear and uncertainty among our community, and worldwide. People are behaving strangely, such as buying up tremendous amounts of toilet paper, and hoarding food and other supplies. While witnessing this behavior I asked my darling wife Vanessa, "What is the relationship between surrender and ongoing health and wellbeing?" She had an immediate answer, based on her love of solutions and her dislike of going over and over the problems.

Vanessa's response was:

"The formula for health and well-being is:

1. Face denials.
2. Become aware of, and practice, acceptance of suppressed emotions.
3. Give your weaknesses to God.
4. Be willing to receive God's grace, and replacement of weaknesses with strengths."

I love her answer, and when I read it, I responded that this is related to Baba's statement: "Do your best. Then, don't worry. Be happy in my love. I will help you." Because the journey of health and well being is partially a journey of right effort, and partially a result of our karma from past lives, and our impressions, as well as our genetic makeup (or DNA). So it is quite complex. I love that Vanessa brings into this conversation the role of the repressed (or suppressed) emotion. A whole book could be written on that subject alone.

I also asked my dear friend, and spiritual sister, Ms. Julie Engsberg, DMQ, the same question. [2]

Julie's Response:

> "Building trust in the Master in order to surrender can bring greater peace. Surrender can lead to new activities given by the Master which challenge one and therefore new stresses can be encountered. It cannot be expected to gain lasting health, or continuous peace. But to resign to the Master's work in our lives will bring a sense of confidence and a unity of being.
>
> "Speaking from my own experience, trust in the Master is of paramount importance to the potentiality of surrender. This has been a process for me. To know for myself that the Master is who He says He is – to have conviction – has been a prerequisite to trust, and trust a prerequisite to surrenderance. Surrender occurs gradually, or in glimpses, and with each glimpse has come joy and peace. As if I had found what I was always looking for (again! After finding Meher Baba).
>
> "More internal changes occurred and I realized that all my aims of peace, joy, health and well-being are secondary to surrender and requesting that the Master guide me in pleasing Him. Pleasing Baba

has been the way of Mehera and other Mandali, letting that prayer be the way to a close relationship with Baba.

"Guided in my life, I am currently using the thought process or way of being known as the "provisional ego". As Baba is doing all through a person in this practice, it is a surrender of one's own attachment (again in glimpses) to one's actions and their results. Why not surrender all, this life and this body, future lives and the journey, knowing the Master has it all in his hands? Glimpses of his majesty, authority, Satchidananda (Truth, Knowledge, and Bliss), his humor and his infinite personality are a great inner joy. He guides on through brief or sometimes lasting experiences which reinforce the practice of the provisional ego on my journey.

"I can begin to understand a truth and incorporate it into my life. Also I may understand through transmission of a Truth. Although such gems may appear on a journey, let me emphasize that He is the gift. The Master leads and glimpses of surrender bring one to a closer relationship with Him. Joy, Peace, and Happiness result from this relationship, not from any accomplishment of the mind."

Regarding the role of surrender in hardship and adversity, Meher Baba explained in his message "The Seven Realities":

> The only Real Surrender is that in which the poise is undisturbed by any adverse circumstances, and the individual, amidst every kind of hardship, is resigned with perfect calm to the will of God. [3]

If you contrast Meher Baba's "Real Surrender" with the sign in the restaurant in Arizona, it is clear to me that both are speaking about the use of self-will, and the relationship to God's Will. How else could one become "resigned with perfect calm to the will of God," unless the ego surrenders self will, and realizes that the will of God is best? Naturally, the restaurant sign only implies this relationship. Regarding the relationship of surrender to hardship and adversity, it reminds me of the message from Baba known as "My Wish," in which he states:

> Be resigned to every situation and think honestly and sincerely: "Baba has placed me in this situation." [4]

This sure sounds like surrender to me, and in fact it goes beyond active surrender as we think that Baba is the one putting us in the situation, for the best. Although I rarely know what is best for me, I have full faith that Baba knows and is always doing what is best for me. Knowing that all Baba does for me is ultimately for the best, I can more easily surrender into, and breathe into what is next. Does this mean I don't resist? No. There are many times when my ego is resisting this surrender, and that is why this is a spiritual path, and not a spiritual light switch. I can't just switch my ego off, and suddenly be enlightened. But, like a dimmer switch, I can become brighter, and slowly more brighter. With Baba, I can move closer, step by blessed step, to him.

Before ending this section, I was reminded recently of an experience I had which is another aspect of surrender, and shows how multifaceted this whole topic really is. I discussed the story with Aspen, and she felt it definitely should be included in this book, so here it is:

This took place in Arizona around 2005. I was renting an office space in the basement of an old brick building in downtown Flagstaff. My office had no windows, it was more like a cave. It had one air vent, but it was inexpensive, and I just needed a place to focus so I could work. One day, during the summer time, it got incredibly hot in the office, and I tried to figure out how to make air come out of the vent, to cool down. I couldn't figure it out, so I called the landlord, we will call him "Perry."

Perry said he didn't know and to look some more. I got some tools and took the vent cover off the vent so I could see where the air came from. Upon inspection, I saw that the vent shaft was cut, and that it was covered by the ceiling, and the floorboards from the next level up in the building. In other words, it may have been a vent at one point, but it was completely non-functional now. I called Perry back, and told him what I found. He said, something like, "Well that's just the way it is." When he said that, I felt contracted, and got a profound sense of fear in my body. The call ended.

I am normally not a fearful person, and I was surprised at my fear and triggered state. I went home from work, and that night I had a bad dream. In my dream I was a Chinese worker, and my landlord Perry was in my dream too, only he was Chinese and he was my boss. In the dream I desperately needed my job, because I had a family, and couldn't afford to be unemployed. As my Chinese boss, Perry had mistreated me badly because he knew I needed the job, but I didn't have the courage to speak up, and I lived in fear. It felt more like a past life memory than a dream. When I woke, I knew that to finish that unresolved karma, I had to speak up to Perry directly in this lifetime.

I went to work that morning with renewed clarity and fiery passion. Upon arrival I promptly called the City of Flagstaff, Planning and Zoning Commission. The fellow at the city office was extremely kind to me as I explained my situation, and so I asked him, "Is there an actual law about landlords needing to provide adequate ventilation?" He immediately said, "Yes, people need to breathe." He offered to give me the volume number and the page number where I can find the law, in the library. He also asked who my landlord was and what the address was, but I didn't provide that information. I needed to wait.

I went to the library, found the book of laws, and made a photocopy of the specific page with the rental space ventilation details. Then I wrote a cover letter to Perry, and attached the law, with highlighting on the part of the page that was pertinent. I dropped off the letter with his secretary and waited.

Before long, my phone rang. It was Perry. I gathered my courage and said, "I need a vent which works, and which will provide me air, it is too hot in here." And he said, "That's going to have to be on your dime." He had the tone of an empowered man who didn't have to listen to me. He made it clear that he refused to pay for it. I responded, "Well, I called the City of Flagstaff Planning and Zoning and they gave me a reference to the law which states you must provide adequate ventilation. I attached that law to a letter I wrote to you. It is not going to be "on my dime," because you are required by law to provide this for me. I didn't tell the city who you are, and where this office is, but if you don't provide ventilation I will discuss this again with the city." The call ended and I didn't know what would happen.

The next morning there were two construction workers at my office, drilling a hole about five inches diameter through the thick brick wall at the back of my office directly out to the alley which ran the length of the building. They then proceeded to fit it with a pipe, a blower fan, and a variable speed switch, a filter, and a hood on the outside. I was thrilled, and I could breathe. Every time I saw Perry after that, he nodded to me and spoke respectfully, starting with, "Hello, Laurent." I knew the karma had been resolved. What does this story have to do with surrender? Did I live up to Baba's wish, that I "be resigned," and feel that Baba "has placed me in this situation" as he said?

Well, I guess this is one of those cases where, instead of surrendering to a toxic landlord, I focused on my self-care and wellbeing, and stood up for what was best. Spiritually, it was best for all of us, and whomever came after me renting that office.

Chapter Thirteen: Experience

Throughout this book, I have provided examples of the ways that I have learned about the process of surrender, and the ways that I have applied these lessons to my personal spiritual journey. However, I have avoided discussion about some difficult situations I have faced which severely tested my faith. These situations mostly involved relationships with important people in my life including my father, my first wife, my children, and even professional relationships at work. These situations deeply triggered my ego to react in sometimes less than spiritual ways. Aspen was the one who encouraged me to write about these situations in this volume, to make myself more vulnerable and in her words, to describe my "emotional process," which she rightly said I had never done. I will therefore narrate how beloved Baba helped me navigate my father's suicide (even before I knew his name), and subsequently my divorce, some issues about marriage in general, my own fatherhood, and finally getting terminated from contract work in 2019.

My Father's Suicide

Before now, the only time I've written about my father's suicide was in the book *The Doorbell of Forgiveness,*[1] and that was in the context of forgiving my father for his act of killing himself. I have never contemplated this in terms of surrender, however my darling daughter Aspen has asked me to write about this in relation to surrender, so I will.

This morning, as I woke, I was reminded of that tragic time over thirty years ago, and remembered to add here that roughly a month before my father took his life, I had a premonitory dream:

> I was with my father in his art studio in our apartment, on the 10th floor of our building, and which had three large windows. He opened the middle of the three windows and climbed out onto the ledge. He put his hands together in prayer, or diving pose, and jumped. I rushed to the window and looked down. Where he would have landed was a large lake, with people in and around the lake. I rushed down ten stories, and there was a police car waiting for me on the street in front of the building, and the police told me to get in the car. I went with them, but they started driving away from the lake. I said, "No, turn around it is back that way..." and I pointed to where the lake was behind us. They turned the car, and headed to the lake. When we reached the shore, I opened the door and got out and I woke up.

At that time of his suicide, I was sixteen, and attending high school in New York City. My sister, Sarah, is four years older than me, so she was finished with high school, and working, and looking into college. My mother was the bread-winner, and always working, at that time in the fashion industry on Seventh Avenue. As fate would have it, the dream was almost exact. He did jump from the building, but used the roof (13th floor). There was no lake, but there was a police car taking my mother and me to the building. Amazing. Now I feel that I had the dream so that I would be prepared, and could be more present to help my mother with her suffering.

Contemplating it now, what did I have to surrender in this process around my father's suicide? Well, the first thing that comes to mind is that I was still a child, or young man. As a result of his suicide, I feel I surrendered my childhood. I gave up childish ways of looking at life, and suddenly became much more serious.

I remember that it was a gradual process, and it was not "clean" or defined, but rather started with a deep sense of detachment from life. I was so shocked by the sudden change that I became a witness to my own life, and in that witnessing things appeared differently to me. For example, sitting in high school taking a spelling test seemed absurd to me, like beyond-silly, to the point of meaninglessness. I thought – what am I doing here? Why should I be sitting here like this? Who cares how to spell these words? I sure didn't care. But it went much deeper, I started to not care about a lot of things, and conversely, I started caring about other things, new things. I started to wonder – Does my father have a soul? Where did he "go." He's gone – as in, I can't see him (death is like that). But is he really gone? Where does anyone go after death? Do we return? What about reincarnation? Things like that. Slowly this not caring about some things, and caring more about other things and new things took the form of me actually looking around my own apartment, where I had grown up all my life, differently. I started to look at my surroundings. For example, rather than take it all for granted, I started to read the spine of every book on every shelf, to see what was around me. I found a book on meditation, by Eknath Easwaran, and read it. [2]

I even started to meditate, based on his instructions in the book. This was all extremely new. As a teen growing up in Manhattan, I had never meditated a day in my life, and had no interest in spirituality before that. Years later, and after I "came to Baba," I picked up that meditation book again and smiled when I saw that he not only spoke about Meher Baba in that book, but he met Baba in India while he was in university. Such a small world.

Then I started to become more interested in spiritual things, and less interested in my past, and previous behaviors, such as going out drinking with my friends, and smoking marijuana, etc. In fact, I remember that a number of surrenders happened in a row, in relatively quick succession. I read a book by a Buddhist monk, and he admonished me to give up sarcasm. I read his description of sarcasm and deeply identified with that behavior, so I made a sincere effort to be less sarcastic. Next, I started to drink less alcohol. This was partly because my father was an alcoholic, and partly because I thought it was more spiritual to drink less. While I never knew my father drunk, as he gave up drinking cold turkey when I was young, my sister and mother did know him drunk, and that made a deeply negative impression on the family.

Finally, once I learned about Meher Baba, and found out he said, "No drugs," I gave up marijuana. I smoked one last time telling Baba as I smoked - that's it Baba, I am done. That was in 1986 and I have never smoked again, over thirty years later.

Shortly after this, I saw that Baba was extremely serious about no sex outside of marriage. I had a girlfriend at that time who was slightly older than me. Naturally, she was interested in our sexual experience together, but I told her that since I am with Meher Baba, I would not be having sex unless we were married. I knew this would be surprising, yet she tolerated it to some extent. By which I mean that she asked if we could have children together, which I interpreted as marriage, and when I said no, she ended up cheating on me with another fellow. I didn't find out about the infidelity until years later, after we had broken up. When I did hear about it, I wasn't really that surprised but a little disappointed. I must have been an odd and difficult boyfriend. The point is, I surrendered sexual experience, instead promising Baba I would wait until I was married, to please him. And I did wait.

Back to the question of my father's suicide. At some point, my mother found a boyfriend, and he moved in. That was the day I moved out, and I guess some part of me surrendered my childhood home to another man. A man I happened to like, thank God, but a man not of my own blood, not my father, and just a man who was now with my mother. I left gracefully, no fuss, and found a room for rent in my friend's apartment in Queens. This felt freeing and completely different. Aspen asked me in what way this was freeing. I think that, growing up in Manhattan, and the types of behaviors my parents exhibited, it was not particularly peaceful or centered. I must have been internalizing a lot of traumatic, and other types of experiences, which once I had my own apartment had me feeling like I was on an inflated "inner-tube" laying in the sun, floating around in my own space, no one coming or going, just me being on my own path, living my life fully with Baba. I loved that feeling.

I will end this section sharing the final surrender from that period that comes to mind. I had a small atomic family growing up. Just me and my sister and our parents. We had some cousins but they were not that close either physically or emotionally. I felt closest to my cousin Andrea, but she didn't seem to like Baba, and we drifted apart. That left just me and my sister and mother. I felt that for my own self-care I had to detach more and more. Of course, at sixteen I didn't use the phrase self-care, but that is what my detachment was. I felt I needed to surrender my mother and sister to Baba, to give them to him, and become truly free. That was not so easy, since we all lived in the New York City area.

I made up my mind, and with a tremendous effort, prayed hard for them both, and then quit my job, and moved from New York to Myrtle Beach, South Carolina to live near the Meher Spiritual Center. That was in early 1991. I was twenty-two years old at that time. I had an extremely good job in New York at a grant foundation, and was well connected, so my friends and family thought I had completely lost my mind. Someone actually said to me out loud that they thought I had been, "... brainwashed by Meher Baba." I just laughed, and responded, "Do you know what you are saying?" How could I explain my new life? I couldn"t, so I didn't try. I just left. I surrendered my old community and my old life. Now, decades later, almost no one from that period remains a real friend.

The Divorce

Have you ever been stepped on by an elephant? I have been.

I knew when this first sentence came to me about my divorce that I would risk sounding like a victim, and that is a sound I dislike. I also know that when my daughter asked me to be more vulnerable in my writing, to share my feelings, and my process around my feelings, that I would have to explain the elephant incident. Meher Baba has warned us against backbiting, and I don't want to throw anyone under the bus, so I will have to be hyper-mindful when telling this story. Here is how I remember it.

Shortly before this start of this story, the two most supportive people in my life, Don Stevens, and my uncle Dieter Jacobs, both passed away rather rapidly. By rapidly I mean a couple of months after an indication that they were in serious health trouble. I felt I could only lean on Meher Baba directly, at that point. My friends were extremely confused about the divorce. Some left me, some remained, some were just trying to figure out what was happening.

I moved out of our family home on the day after Christmas 2011, after eighteen years of marriage and two children, a son named Cyprus, and a daughter named Aspen, at the time ages five and sixteen respectively. Suffice it to say that I had reached the point where, after three marriage counselors, and nine months of trying to put Humpty-dumpty back together again after a crippling betrayal, I no longer wanted the marriage, at all. I simply wanted to be free. When I walked out the door, I had no idea what I was doing. I knew only what I was not doing, I was not going to stay there any longer. I never went back. Surrender in divorce is worthy of an entire book, and yet I will try to reduce it to a chapter here.

I rented a three bedroom home in a neighborhood as close as possible to my daughter's high school, in hopes that she would see my efforts, and spend more time with me during this painful process. I felt if she was near to her school, it would be easier to settle in with me. The three bedrooms therefore were to create one for her, one for her brother, and one for me. I believed that I could create a happy and healthy environment for them both, for the times they would be with me, and I set about doing it in earnest. This gave me direction. I also felt that I shouldn't miss any work. In the entire process, I only missed a few days of work; when I was on-site at a client in Texas, and heard some shocking news from a friend. I felt that with only a few days of missed work, I was doing great. The only problem was, I couldn't get out of bed. I mean, I couldn't stand up because there was an elephant standing on my chest.

Of course it was not a physical elephant, but the emotional experience of starting my new life, all over again from scratch, after eighteen years of creating a family with a partner and two beautiful children was so profoundly painful, that the only way I can describe it – even years later – is that the foot of an elephant was pressing my body down into my bed, and I couldn't move. Another version of this, related but different, is that I would wake up from sleep, and for the first time in my life – my waking experience was a nightmare, and I was only finding peace in sound sleep. It was as if my unconscious experience was becoming much more preferable to my awake life. I had never experienced this, and it was distressing to me.

As Lily Tomlin said, "It's going to get worse, before it gets worse." That is what happened. I spent the first half of 2012 in some type of deep shock. I didn't eat much, I drank a lot of wine, but I didn't get drunk. I know this because my ex-wife commented on it, sort of congratulating me, saying, "You know in all that we went through and the painful process of separation and divorce, you never got drunk." I hadn't realized it, no. I was surprised to hear it actually – now, thinking about it, I believe it was out of my deep fear of becoming like my father, who was an alcoholic, that I kept my sense of moderation.

My daughter, for a litany of reasons I won't discuss here, only stayed in her new room at my house a few times during that year. Everyone moved out of the family home ultimately, and she ended up living with her mother, well over ten miles south of her school, in another town. I didn't understand – why would she make that choice? She would visit me briefly and say things like, "I am worried about you Daddy, you don't smile any more." And just show her love and care, but not stay. I arranged for mediation, and got half of the time with my young son in our Parenting Plan, so it was like two weeks with me, and then two weeks with his mother. That was super strange, and I hated this splitting his time up. But what else could we do. We kept experimenting with how much time with each of us, going down to a week on and a week off, but it never felt right, ever. It just felt broken.

My son was extremely confused and angry. He would fly into rages. Who could blame him?

I didn't know how to handle all of the new patterns, and changes, so I focused on work. I remember one of the first surrenders that came up during this period, and it had to do with Aspen's comment, that I never smile any more. I thought – Hmmmm, Baba wants us to be more cheerful, I should try to appear more cheerful, even if I am not feeling it. So, I made an extreme effort that, whenever I would leave the house, I would smile more, and not let anyone know how I was feeling. Just to put on a happy cheerful front. I had no idea if it was working, until I went to get my haircut for work. I spent a lot of time with professional clients, so I feel it is important to look neat and trim. As I was getting my haircut, at a place I knew well from many years of patronage, the stylist in the next booth over said, "It is always so good to see you, you are always so cheerful!" That's when I knew it was working.

Shortly after that, the same stylist confided in me that her husband had betrayed her, and we commiserated. I decided, under the circumstances, to be real and let her know I felt her pain and could empathize. Those were intense days, indeed.

So what was that surrender? It was surrendering self-pity, and wanting acknowledgment for my suffering from my community. As Baba would have it, I was given a job offer to become a Director at a startup in Silicon Valley. I had recently started a new relationship, my first real "girlfriend" in about twenty years, so we discussed it together carefully. She encouraged me, saying it would be best for everyone if we left that town in

Arizona, and went West to make a new life. Honestly, that was the single most difficult decision of my adult life.

I knew that accepting the role at the start up would mean less time with my children. I knew I had no idea what I was doing. I prayed to Baba about it. I spoke to the few remaining friends I had about it all, and it was a kaleidoscope of issues and advice. At the end of the day I knew it was my decision to make. If I stayed I would not be able to take the new role at the start up, a missed opportunity I wasn't sure I could afford to miss. If I left for California, I would have to surrender and sacrifice time with my children, and perhaps, depending on how they experienced this, my relationship with my children. I decided to go.

For the next nine months, I would drive from San Francisco to Flagstaff, Arizona – fourteen hours each way, to spend a weekend a month with my kids. I only missed one month, for reasons I don't want to discuss here. After nine months, I arranged with my ex-wife to move with me to Oregon, so we could co-parent our son there. At first she said no, because she couldn't afford to move. I asked – If I pay for you and your boyfriend to move, would you then move? She agreed. A week after the move, my girlfriend shocked me when she left to return to Arizona. Apparently she couldn't stand living in Oregon, and wanted to be closer to her mother. Co-parenting in Oregon was much better. I got on a weekend visitation schedule with Cyprus, and the anger in him slowly began to subside. Aspen was by now in college in Arizona, so that was a-whole-nother journey, and can't be described here.

In 2016 I got married to Vanessa, and shortly thereafter moved to North Carolina to start a new life with her there. That was the most recent surrender, as having just gotten things on track in Oregon I felt the need to focus on my new marriage, and creating a healthy home. Why North Carolina? What I can say, wholeheartedly and with certainty, is that now in 2020, with eight years of hindsight since the divorce, I do feel I made the right decisions.

Aspen and I have become closer than ever, after a tremendous amount of work on these issues. And Cyprus asked his mother to spend a year, "living with Dad." He is now thirteen, and he has been with us in Wilmington since July 10, 2019. By Baba's Grace, and our efforts, so far we have been having an incredible journey in surrender. I am happier than ever with my new marriage, and a blended family.

Marriage in General

Starting with marriage, I can say it is one of the most fertile fields possible for opportunities to surrender, and this topic could be a book unto itself. The tricky part of this is that naturally, it doesn't make sense that everything your partner wants should be a time to surrender to such a desire. No, of course not. On the other hand, it is not never the case either, there is some balance of knowing when it is time to surrender and when not. It is a bit like general martial arts: knowing when to advance, when to hold your ground, and when to retreat. Or as in Aikido, knowing when to enter, and knowing when to strike.

If it was a simple as, "always agree" to whatever your spouse says, marriage would be much easier to navigate. Neither is it right, from my point of view, to equate all desires or wants with God's Will. So, how in the heck can we navigate all of these issues. I think there are many aspects of surrender in marriage that will appear, perhaps more and more as one matures in the give and take of love, but that the goal of marriage should be to focus on making your partner happy, even at the cost of your own happiness. This rapidly brings us back into the discussion of deficient, healthy, and toxic surrender. If what my partner is asking for is not what I want, but helping to create that, or allowing that, is something I can live with because it makes her happy, that is a type of surrender. Of course sometimes the situation is much more complicated than this, and it could be about a belief, or a child, or a business venture, or whatever, and there may be strong emotions mixed into the whole thing. Let me tell a story which may elucidate one of my most difficult marriage surrenders.

It was during the wedding planning, and we both were creating our lists of guests to invite. Then once we each had a sense of who, we shared our lists with each other to create the final list. She had one person on her list who, how can I best say this – wasn't the last person in the world I wanted at our wedding, but maybe the second to the last. I couldn't believe she even requested this person attend. From that point it was hours, days, weeks, and I believe we even got our relationship therapist involved in helping to resolve the issue, as it was just an extremely tight knot to untie, fraught with triggers, and pain and other problems. In any case, we were in a stalemate. Nothing was moving. We were stuck. How to get unstuck?

I pleaded, I begged, I don't want our wedding marred by the presence of this person, and my having to endure their presence and then remember them after the event. No movement.

I surrendered.

Okay, invite them. That part of the wedding, their presence, didn't go well, but we all survived. It made my wife happy, even at the cost of my own happiness.

Meher Baba said, "To love those whom you cannot love, is to love me as I should be loved." This was one of those situations, and it was extraordinarily difficult for me. And why? Because my ego had so many reasons why it was a bad idea to invite this person. I had many justifications for my feelings. I could get almost anyone who heard my reasons to agree with me in a matter of minutes, and I knew I was right. By God, why couldn't my fiancé see that?! That is the voice of the ego. And apparently another voice, the one that was less ego, and perhaps closer to Baba and Truth said, "Okay, invite them."

Fatherhood and Surrender

Depending upon how you count, I have five children.

I say "depending" because I have two children from my first marriage, when I remarried my wife had three from her previous marriage, and one of the five is – how can I say this, not really in my life. So, if I was to write this properly, it would be at least five chapters, one for each "child." My oldest is Aspen, she is twenty something and living in her own home on the East Coast. Three of them are living at home with us in North Carolina. And one, yes the one that is not really in my life, lives somewhere nearby in North Carolina also.

I am tempted to give one example for each child regarding surrender, and then call this topic done.

Aspen

Well, since she is the one who asked me to create this chapter and she is also my editor, I am going to speak freely, and if she doesn't like it, she can edit it right out of the book. When I got divorced from Aspen's mother it was the lowest point in my life. I told them both, this is more painful to me than my father's suicide. Aspen asked me, why? My ex-wife just got angry at me for saying that. My response to Aspen was, "Because I care more deeply for you, and our family, then I did for my own father." That was and is the truth. Unfortunately for me, at that time, I experienced Aspen taking a side in the divorce, and that side was with her mother. At the time, I had no idea what was happening to me. I thought I was going to completely lose my mind. To have my own family fall apart in such a dramatic fashion – not only did I never imagine it – but now that it was occurring, I didn't know how I could survive. Anguish, and massive confusion, and then depression rushed in. I had to surrender my relationship with my own child not knowing whether it would ever return. I did surrender and it did return, years later, better than ever.

Cyprus

Because Cyprus was so small when I got divorced – and because of all I had found out in divorce about what to say, and not to say to the children, I decided to not explain to Cyprus why I was divorcing his mother. What would I be able to say to my five year old son about reasons for divorce, which could possibly help him? Nothing. I decided to stick to not speaking badly about his mother in his presence, ever, and just trust that one day it will all make sense. At the time, it didn't even all make sense to me, so pretending I could have it make sense to others was out of the question. What I didn't expect was how angry he would become. This was based, at least in part, on his blaming me for the divorce. Naturally, to him I was responsible for the breakup of the marriage and family. It sure looked that way, since I left the house, never went back and then divorced his mother. When asked by him, year after year, "Why?" I would say, when you are eighteen I will explain it all. He never liked that. He used to say, "Fine, then I will ask my sister!" I had to surrender his blaming me, and the anger he felt towards me. I had to give up wanting to control his feelings, and that it was not my fault. I had to allow him the dignity to have his beliefs, his feelings, his judgment of me, regardless of how true or untrue that may be.

Vanessa's Children

I have to be incredibly careful here not to offend anyone, so I may get more and more "anonymous' as we go. When Vanessa and I married, we both became "step parents' or "bonus parents' as some say, and that brought with it a ton of lessons for me. Her children didn't choose me, she did. Why should they like me at all? They didn't seem to at first, so we had a long journey of getting to know each other. At the time this journey of having "bonus sons' started six years ago they were ages 3, 15, and 17. Paradoxically for me, the one I felt the most kinship with is the one with whom I had the biggest fight and I rarely see him at all.
The other two live with us currently.

So, to generalize, I can say the surrender lessons with these boys has to do with my desire to control. I can't control what they do, but I can set boundaries regarding what they are allowed to do in our new home. I can't control the values they have chosen to embrace, but if those values are illegal, or harmful to themselves or others, I can speak up. I can reprimand, and give consequences and make my best efforts to reform them. This is all made more complicated by the fact that these boys already have a father, so what do they need from me? Well, if they are living with me, they must need something. So, I do my best to balance what I perceive they need, with what I feel I need for this to be a healthy relationship.

I can surrender my desire to control their actions, and values, with the understanding that I am going to teach the youngest one manners if he is having meals at our dining room table. I can surrender what happens outside the home, with the understanding that if someone is inside our home they must treat Vanessa and me with respect and dignity at all times. I don't have to be a victim, just as no one has to put up with a situation where their surrender has become toxic. I can change the circumstances, with my voice, or my actions. This is perhaps an abstract way of speaking, but it is as close as I can come to the issues without getting into airing dirty laundry and I'm not going to that right now.

Adopted Children

At the time Vanessa started her divorce in 2014, there were two teenagers which she said she had "adopted" - meaning they were living with her at her family home. When her divorce was final, she and I immediately got engaged. This is a complicated situation, since the two teenagers also had birth parents who were still living. This brings up a good story about surrender, which I think will round out this chapter. I knew both the teenagers, and I liked them. During our engagement both teenagers left Vanessa, one went back to her mother in the midwest, and the other stayed locally at her friend's home nearby. As a new couple we made plans to move in together, into an apartment. She wanted the teen who was local at the friend's house to move in with us, and I agreed to the one. The other had already moved back to her mother, so that was off the table for me. As we started to look for places to live, and before we were married, my fiancé said that she invited the other teen to come live with us at the new apartment for the summer. I was shocked.

From my point of view, I was starting a new marriage, in a new home, and had already surrendered to one of the teens coming to live with us, but now – without asking me, she had invited the other. I was upset. When I brought this up, we just fought about it, and it just got worse. Should I surrender again, and now start a new marriage with two adopted teens, and three bonus sons, all in one home? It sounded like madness to me. I held my ground and said, "No." We fought and fought and it never resolved, so I said forget it, we are not moving in together and I retreated. Eventually, and by that I mean months later, we found a condominium for rent by the beach, during the off-season which is cheaper. We moved in together there with only one child, the youngest. Her two oldest stayed with her ex-husband nearby. The adopted children never came to live with us, ever. My two children hadn't come to live with us either.

The problem with surrender is, it is just that – surrender. We both had to surrender control over what others would and would not do, including each other. I could go on and on about this, but I will leave it at that. Fatherhood and surrender is difficult work, and I have the gray hairs to prove it.

Edge Energy

During November and early December of 2019, I had to navigate some of the most intense waters of my adult life. There was some intense political drama at the firm where I was consulting as a Tech Lead. My immediate manager actually said out loud to me, "Laurent, it is because you are so successful that there is a target on your back." I responded in shock, saying it should be the opposite, that people should be supportive of success, but he indicated that was not the Edge culture.

After working extraordinarily hard for more than seven months, on a six month contract, the result was that they loved the software development work, and I was personally thanked for it, however they decided not to renew three of the consulting contracts. I was one of the three. I can say – That's business, however the impact of this was huge. I had to immediately figure out what to do next, during the Thanksgiving and Christmas holidays, which are not periods to start a new role, in my line of work. Since I had been working on this book, Surrender with Meher Baba during that same period when I was at that firm, I decided the best thing for me to do - rather than panic – would be to surrender to Meher Baba, just like I was recommending in this book, and Baba was telling us (and which I was quoting all over in this book).

In other words, I knew it was time to walk my own talk about surrender. I went down to the beach with Vanessa, to pray. I would silently surrender, and also ask Baba in prayer to guide us. In so many ways, in his bedroom in Myrtle Beach, in the Lagoon Cabin at the Meher Spiritual Center, at the ocean's edge at Wrightsville Beach near our home, I would offer Baba my family, myself, my livelihood, my ability to provide, my career, my past - present - and future, my children, my wife, all I was all I am and all I will be, and the blood of my own body. It may sound dramatic, but I was digging into the depths of my heart to really hold up, with both hands up, and outstretched to Baba everything, asking only for his guidance and love, and grace. Naturally, I knew from my many years with Baba, that he also asked us, "Do your best. Then don't worry, be happy. I will help you." Doing my best took the form of my posting two highly technical blogs about Python and Java programming with Big Data, and Apache Kafka Streaming, and things like that. I then shared my work with dozens of contacts, and told my friends and colleagues I am looking for my next project. It is quite difficult to explain here in words how vulnerable, scared, and hopeless I felt – not knowing.

Having a wife and kids relying upon you, and not knowing how it will work out, is an excruciating time of having to depend wholly and solely on God to provide. Since Meher Baba is my God, I prayed to Baba and re-surrendered my life, and all of our lives at his divine feet. The only thing I felt I did know (and do know) is how I feel about Baba. And I know it is on me to surrender to him. As He once said, "Love is a gift from God to man. Obedience is a gift from Master to man. And surrender is a gift from man to Master." While I didn't look upon my surrender as a gift, I did take it seriously and practiced it repeatedly, multiple times a day, over about three weeks. The most recent results I have been experiencing in my life after processing this surrender is how many people have communicated to me their wish to help me or hire me. It is astounding. I don't want to say it is a result of surrender, because that may seem to cheapen it and be somehow misleading. All I can say is I am now trying to figure out which of the offers to accept, and praying for Baba to guide me regarding which is the right offer for our family. There is an abundance-downpour after the drought.

Retrospective

Now that I am over fifty years old, I can look back on five decades of experience and evaluate, perhaps too subjectively, a little of where I have been on this surrender path. From zero to sixteen years old, I was nowhere at all on this path. I was, like most kids in New York, not interested in spirituality, or religion. Growing up in the artistic and intellectual circles of my friends and family, surrender was not even in my vocabulary - other than the stereotypical white flag of defeat in battle. With the passing of my father, and my "coming to Baba," that rather suddenly shifted, and from seventeen to say twenty eight, so the next ten years, I can honestly say that surrender started and I was in the early years of trying to surrender. But I had no real idea of how to do that, or what I was doing, other than that it was an aspect of my love for Baba, and that my love and obedience were connected to surrender. I didn't spend much time thinking about surrender, just trying to love Baba. As He said, "Let your life itself be my message of love and truth to others." I was just trying to live my path, plain and simple. Right around when I turned twenty-eight my entire life shifted to the South West, based in Flagstaff, Arizona, and that is where the surrender started appearing in more earnest, culminating in the loss of my mentors, and my marriage and family life, and the deep reliance upon Baba directly.

When I left Arizona for California and Oregon in the winter of 2012-2013, I would have been around forty-four, and the surrender lessons started coming faster, although I didn't discuss this with anyone, and I wasn't consciously researching or linking my experience to surrender. I was just doing it. Then in 2017, just a few years ago, this got kicked into the highest gear with the request for me to facilitate the Surrender with Meher Baba seminar. Naturally, when creating a seminar, I didn't want to be a hypocrite, so I practiced surrender more and more in my own life, before sitting with others as a facilitator of this topic. Even then, the "impostor syndrome" we hear so much about, was creeping in, with my inner voice asking, do you really know anything about surrender? As Baba would have it, I guess I do know a little.

Contemplating where I am today around surrender, while writing this book, I can say that surrender has become less of an act, meaning an activity, and more of my way. I don't mean to say I have in any way mastered surrender in my life, but in the spirit of Martin Luther King, Jr. when he said, "Forgiveness is not an occasional act, it is a constant attitude," I feel that in my life opportunities for surrender are extremely numerous. They probably have always been plentiful, and I am just more sensitive to my opportunity to surrender, and so it has become more of my daily living attitude and less of an occasional act.

Aspen asked me, "What is your next step in surrender?" You know, I have never thought of this. I'm not sure that steps are how I relate to surrender. I was just reminded, while contemplating this question, of a story. Maybe this can elucidate my next step in surrender in a way that makes more sense.

I was once deeply troubled by something someone said about Meher Baba, and so I brought this up with Baba directly, explaining what the person had said about him, and how I felt about it. That part is less important, but the feeling I had was important, and the feeling turned into a burning question, or desire, to know where Baba is right now. So, I prayed, for days and weeks, to Baba asking, "Where are you right now Baba?" I had a sense of urgency around this, a longing, and a yearning. I asked repeatedly each day, day after day, week after week, just like that, "Where are you Baba, right now?"

This was during the Arizona period, and I had arranged for a sweat lodge to be created, during the winter, in the snowy woods near Flagstaff. The fresh snow was pristine, and the lodge was perfect for me. I invited just men to sit with me in the lodge, and it went great. We did four rounds of fiery rocks in lodge, and somewhere in the second half, while focusing on Baba, I heard a response in my heart. The response was not words, but as is most often the case in my experience with Baba, I feel-knowing what he is saying to me. It comes in feelings, that are so clear, that when I put words to it (to share with others) it doesn't do justice to the experience of his presence and communication in my heart.

How I would translate the feeling-knowing of what he said to me is,

> "Try to find Me as a flame at the core of your heart.
> Try to find Me as a fire at the center of your being."

It was incredible, and I knew that my weeks of prayer had been answered. Yet, I hadn't expected any answer. It just came like that in the lodge. After the final round, I came out hot and naked, and ran a few steps and leaped up and forward into the night snow, and landed softly with a thwuffff – completely embedded in many inches of the forest snow near the lodge.

So what does that all mean? Perhaps a way I can see surrender is, the more I turn away from the world and Maya, and the false attractions, and enticements of the ego, the more I can focus on him and his presence within me, and the more I can surrender.

I don't know what the ultimate goal is, but I have heard from Baba that the ultimate goal is to merge consciously into Oneness with him. To do that I need to let go, finally, of all thoughts of "I, my, me, and mine." I believe Baba, and I am striving for that union, in the ways He has shown me are meaningful to me. I don't believe there is – one way, or one path – I believe there are as many paths back to union with him as there are souls in Creation, and I trust that process.

Love to you all who read this.

After reading all these experiences, Vanessa asked me, "What effects did you feel or experience all these surrenders left with you as you walked forward? How did your conversation with God change after these series of surrenders? At what point in your life did you understand consciously that you were engaged in surrender? Did you feel closer to yourself or to God after any particular surrender in your life? Has surrender had an effect on your relationship with God? Have you ever felt a sense of clarity after a surrender that you did not have before? Over time as you have been surrendering things large and small do you experience a shift in your ability to surrender?"

Wow. That is a lot of great questions, let me honor her effort by answering each one below, and then I will move on to the surrender exercises I have prepared for you.

VW: What effects did you feel, or experience, all these surrenders left with you as you walked forward?
LW: Before I knew Baba, a deeper sense of intuition, or trusting myself. And after knowing him, a deeper love connection with Meher Baba in the present moment.

VM: How did your conversation with God change after these series of surrenders?
LW: Before I knew about Meher Baba, God was external and far far away in a place beyond the edge of the Universe. After knowing about Baba, God came closer and closer, and then suddenly but also gradually, by Baba's working and grace in my life, I found him within me.

VW: At what point in your life did you understand consciously that you were engaged in surrender?
LW: Certainly it was after I was involved with Meher Baba, and actively reading everything he wrote including *God Speaks*, and *Discourses*, and other works as well. If you read Baba carefully it is pretty clearly his top priority, and I took this to heart. However, to be honest, I started with the love, and tried to obey, knowing the surrender was and is the hardest part.

VW: Did you feel closer to yourself, or to God, after any particular surrender in your life?
LW: Yes, after each one I felt closer to both myself, and now that I know Baba, closer to God. At the start, I wasn't spiritual enough to know what was going on, but looking back I can say this, every surrender brought me closer to Truth.

VW: Has surrender had an effect on your relationship with God?
LW: Yes, my consciously aware surrender has transformed my relationship with God from an aloof distant uncaring God, to a close intimate relationship with Meher Baba, as the real me.

VW: Have you ever felt a sense of clarity after a surrender that you did not have before?
LW: Definitely, yes. When I had the sweat-lodge answer to my prayer, and got the guidance from Baba about where to find him. That was a great example of clarity. When I had the experience of Baba speaking to me in the Lagoon Cabin about, "Never be afraid to love..." that was amazing clarity. Surrender is a spiritual risk and there are rewards, however it can't be engaged in as a bargain or for the reward otherwise it is not surrender, so it is complex.

VW: Over time as you have been surrendering things, large and small, do you experience a shift in your ability to surrender?"
LW: Yes, I do. The more I practice, I feel the more easily I am able to surrender. I have no idea if that is true, or if I am deluded, but it sure feels like I have been exercising a spiritual muscle and I am getting stronger with my surrender practice. Does that make any sense?

"Avatar Meher Baba" by Vanessa Weichberger, 1997

Chapter Fourteen: Surrender Exercises

When facilitating the Surrender with Meher Baba seminar, we used some of the time to have "surrender exercises' which, according to the feedback I received from the attendees, was quite fruitful. I tend to work best with questions, so I asked them a few questions, and broke the larger group of people into self-organizing groups of two or more. Feel free to try these at home.

Exercise 1

Meher Baba said: "The only Real Surrender is that in which poise is undisturbed by any adverse circumstance, and the individual, amidst every kind of hardship, is resigned with perfect calm to the will of God."

Two questions:
A) How do you relate to this reality about surrender?

B) What is your experience of the will of God?

Exercise 2

Meher Baba stated, "Complete surrenderance to the God-man is not possible for one and all. When this is not possible, the other high roads which can eventually win the grace of God are:

1. Loving obedience to and remembrance of the God-man to the best of one's ability;

2. Love for God and intense longing to see Him and be united with Him;

3. Being in constant company with the saints and lovers of God and rendering them whole-hearted service;

4. Avoiding lust, greed, anger, hatred, and the temptations of power, fame, and faultfinding;

5. Leaving everyone and everything in complete external renunciation and, in solitude, devoting oneself to fasting, prayer and meditation;

6. Carrying on all worldly duties with a pure heart and clean mind and with equal acceptance of success or failure, while remaining detached in the midst of intense activity; and

7. Selfless service of humanity, without thought of gain or reward."

Two questions:

A) Are you prepared to completely surrender to Meher Baba? If not, feel free to share with someone you trust about this, or write in your journal.

B) Do any of the "high roads' given by Baba appeal to you, or deeply resonate with you, and why?

Exercise 3

Given the following blank diagram (see below) showing the abstractions of surrender with a "Healthy" state in the middle, and "Deficient," and "Toxic" states on the left and right respectively, can you fill in the diagram with words or other images, to show how you relate to these possible states of surrender? Can you add more detail about what deficient (not enough) surrender feels or looks like? What about toxic surrender (meaning something is not right, and it has become harmful)?

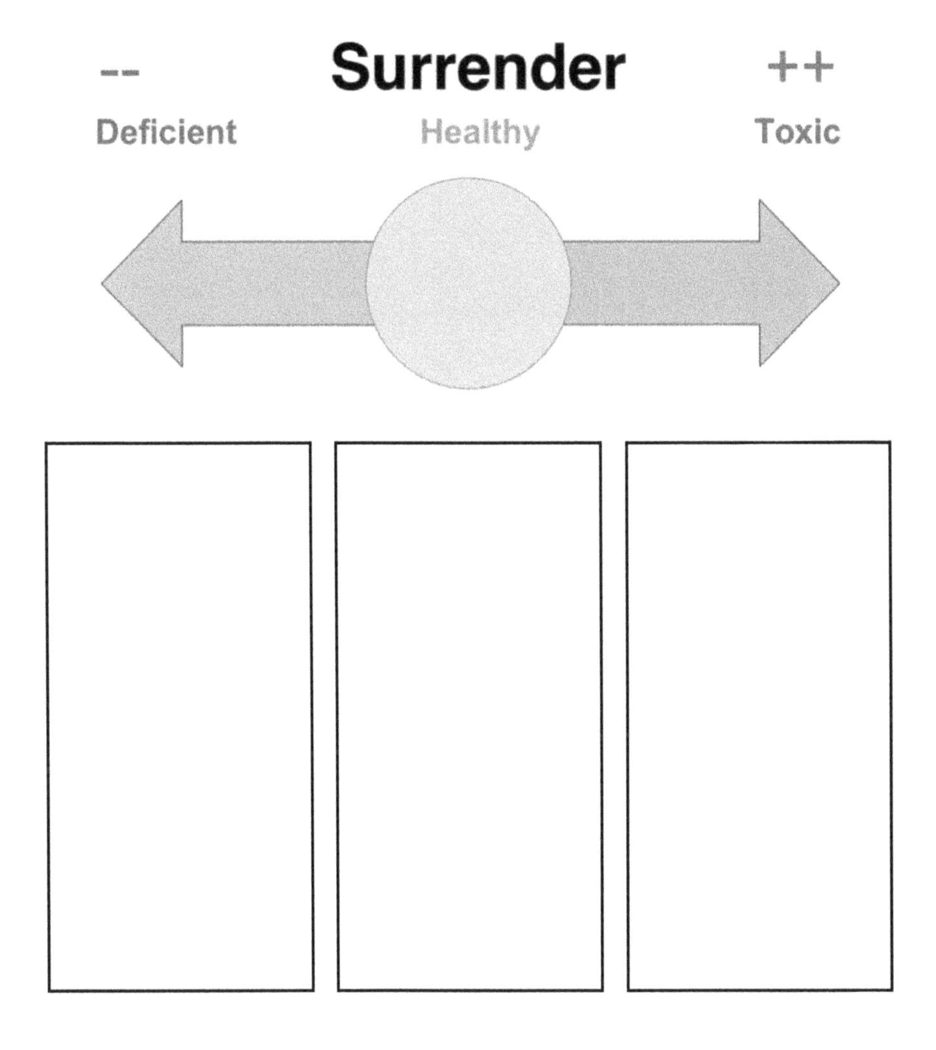

Part II
Contributing Authors

Unworthy

By Evie Lindemann

As my pen pushes across my writing page, I am facing a stark reality. In order to explore both the notion and the practice of surrender, I ask myself about a fundamental belief that I have carried since early childhood. "I am unworthy" is the thought that arises without any prompting and then triggers negative feelings. It likely drove me to become a mental health professional in two different clinical fields, and to train graduate students as a professor of art therapy. Those of us who are drawn to help others often carry issues that we are also looking to resolve. The archetype of the Wounded Healer fits me. This describes a person such as myself who wishes to not only unravel some of the knots in my own psyche, but to also help others unravel theirs. We all carry beliefs about ourselves, some of which are supportive of our growth and others that block us from finding the fundamental beauty residing in our hearts.

If you have ever been chased by a snarling dog, this is the metaphor that best describes how pervasive a belief system can be. It chases us down, takes up lodging in the psyche without paying rent, and creates fear and insecurity. Some examples of beliefs that block us from finding the beauty residing in our hearts are, "I am unimportant," "I am alone," "It is not safe to express my feelings," or "I am invisible." There are scores of these beliefs. When our beliefs tip toward the darker side, it seems to confirm a reality that may simply be a mirage that appears to be fundamentally true. Eventually we must give up all these darker beliefs because they limit our capacities, but until that time it becomes important to work with the contents of our mind. Baba helps us in the sense that when we become closely aligned with Him, he does us the favor of opening up the filtering system that has kept these repositories of our psyche hidden from our awareness. When we become willing to excavate the dark crevices of the psyche, and surrender to the process of self-inquiry, our suffering decreases as our self-awareness expands.

As one Baba lover, put it: "The deep, dark abyss of despair looms large before me at the edge of awareness. Its siren song beckons me to the edge to tumble in. I turn from its mesmerizing pull and, tearing myself away, focus on Meher Baba's love and remain firm in His remembrance and dedication to my mission." In Ray Lee's descriptive words, it is clear that the pull of the abyss is strong and hypnotic and the attraction to that dark despair is so magnetic in nature that it pulls us in. We have all felt that pull, and most of us have fallen into the abyss more than once.

I will describe to you how it was that my convincing feeling of being unworthy led me to a feeling of separateness and isolation, a descent into the abyss, and later to a process of recognizing the value of surrender. I could say that it all began in my early childhood. I could say that my parents were not especially attentive to their five children's needs. I could say that I was not listened to as a child, that my feelings were ignored, that my efforts were not praised, that I felt largely invisible in a family of complex story strands that went back through time to earlier generations who carried traumatic memories that were passed forward. Or I could say that it was all karmic, which it probably was, and that I was the agent of my own choosing of this particular family to work out particular issues. But this seems somewhat harsh and unfeeling, given a topic of delicacy and difficulty. And believing in the law of karmic return did not help me to shake loose from the unworthy core that seemed to occupy the center of my being.

It was, perhaps, the feeling of alienation and separateness that made my passage as narrow and dangerous as it seemed, like the Greek myth of Scylla and Charybdis. As the story goes, the passageway was narrow. On one side stood Scylla, the monster with six heads, ready to devour its victims, and on the other Charybdis, another monster who belched so much water that whirlpools were generated, swallowing up even the most seaworthy vessel. While trying to avoid the one, even the strongest vessel might travel dangerously close to the other and be caught in a whirlpool that swallowed it up. And mine was a very small boat on a tumultuous sea, so that I had no confidence that it was sturdy enough to withstand the assaults of either one of these mythical creatures.

As to the experience of deep alienation and aloneness at the core of my being, I was internally driven by a force that Meher Baba calls divine desperation. I concluded that if this state of aloneness was all that there was, I was not interested in taking part. If, on the other hand, it might be possible that something of value and meaning could be found, then I would risk everything, including my personal safety, to take a deep dive into the unknown. I traveled around the world, starting in European countries, hitchhiked across North Africa, then traveled to a kibbutz in Israel where I flirted with death. My kibbutz had bomb shelters because of our proximity to the Jordanian border, and we were shelled, and sometimes members of the community died. One morning while planting groves of bananas, I got the idea that I should go to India, because by then I knew about Meher Baba, and wondered how to find him in that vast country. I convinced a friend, Richard, whom I met on the kibbutz to accompany me. We traveled overland across the Middle East, and ended up in Afghanistan, waylaid for six months because Richard became deathly ill with foodborne hepatitis. We freely indulged in nearly every kind of psychedelic available and after I worked in Kabul for six months as an illustrator of children's stories for a literacy project, we hit the road again. Good fortune intervened with a letter from Allan Cohen that came to me the day before we left Pakistan for India and Nepal.

Several years before, I had met Allan when I was a student at the University of California, Berkeley. I sought him out for psychotherapy one afternoon, too embarrassed to directly ask for help at the Center. I hid behind some bushes at the Counseling Center, waiting for him to leave after a day's work. He had been described to me by a friend, and I hoped I would choose the right person. As I peered through the bushes a few mental health professionals passed by. Finally, I spotted him. As he crossed my path, I leapt out, likely with a look of desperation on my face. I asked if he were Allan Cohen. When he replied affirmatively, I said: "I need to talk to you." He replied, after dusting himself off a bit, "It looks like you need to talk to me right now."

"Yes," I said, "Yes, I do."

A long therapeutic relationship began, and I could not help but notice the enormous photograph of Meher Baba on the wall behind Allan's chair. Each time I looked at Allan, I had to also look at the photograph. I found it rather annoying that the man in the photograph looked so darn happy, and in comparison, I felt completely miserable. Some months into our sessions, I asked him one day who the guy in the photo was. He told me very briefly about Baba, and our sessions continued. In the early summer of the next year, my family experienced a shattering trauma, the suicide of my father. By now, familiar with Allan and trusting him with my darkest secrets, the nasty poison of my father's death spilled into our sessions. In addition to the anger I felt toward my father for his silences, his depression, and his abandonment of his responsibilities as a parent, I also carried the guilt that in some way I was responsible for his decision, for his desperate act.

While my other four siblings more or less avoided my father because of his seeming aloofness, I did not. We shared some common joys in those earlier years, and he taught me chess, sat by my bedside when I was ill, took me driving out in the country, and played the game of "lost and found" in the cornfields of our family farm. I would hide in the very tall corn plants, and he would always find me. As a young adolescent I began to notice his withdrawal and I took it upon myself to try to pull him out of it. This was clearly not a task for a daughter, but I did not know that at the time. When he killed himself, I felt I had failed him at the same time that he had failed me. His death was the catalyst for my road warrior desperation that took me around the world. I hoped for something better, for something less painful, for something that would provide me with meaning beyond the particularities of my family situation.

With the letter I received at the American Express office in Pakistan, I at last had some instruction on how to find the elusive Meher Baba. Throughout all those months of travel, I never found a single book on Meher Baba, even in the largest Asian cities.

I was getting closer inwardly but needed a few more experiences before I was ready to lay my burden down. Richard and I traveled into Nepal, trekked in the higher elevations of the Himalayas, and went to the sunny coast of Western India to Goa, the hippy haven of South Asia. We lived in a rented shack on the beach, and helped fishermen to bring in their daily catch to procure our dinner. We had a vague plan to visit Meher Baba's home, but in the meantime, we swam, ate fresh fruit, and consumed many hallucinogens in our search for something better. One day on the beach a friend of ours from France told us she had just met a woman who seemed connected to Meher Baba. The woman, Virginia Small, was recovering from a broken leg, hailed from California, and had a small Baba book with her entitled The Advancing Stream of Life. We devoured the book in a single afternoon, looked at each other, and concluded: "Let's get on the steamer tomorrow and head back to Bombay!" I knew nothing about Meher Baba's position on drugs, but somehow, we decided to go to the end of the steamer and drop our entire drug stash, which was sizable, into the Indian Ocean. We did, however, retain two tabs of acid just in case Meher Baba turned out to be a bogus teacher.

By the time we arrived at Meherabad, where we met Meher Baba in His samadhi, and spent time with His mandali, I realized that my long, lonely, and sometimes empty journey had ended with gold. Coming into contact with Meher Baba and His mandali altered my idea of who I was and gave me a penetrating look into meaning and purpose. We flushed those two remaining tabs of acid down an Indian style toilet one hot summer afternoon. If Meher Baba loved me enough to bring me to Him after such a meandering journey, then surely, I must have some worth; that, in fact, I was worthy rather than unworthy. And after that first trip to India, which was a kind of blissful honeymoon between Baba and me, I returned to the West.

But that pervasive sense of unworthiness crept back into my psyche, where it had taken residence early on, and while it seemed quiet on that first pilgrimage, it came back to me with a loud and persistent voice. Then began the "if only I do this," the message about my unworthiness will go away. And so, I embarked on the study of psychology, becoming a mental health professional with my own serious wounding under my belt, and fitting very comfortably into the archetype of the Wounded Healer I mentioned earlier. It required me to find a way to tolerate the sadness and loss that I heard in my clients' stories, ones that echoed some of my own, while learning how to remain steady in the presence of the pain of others.

Our capacity to tolerate and learn from experiences of disappointment, through the shock of sudden endings, through self-negating thoughts, through the loss of control and the realization that there is very little we can control other than how we respond to these indignities, is serious business. As Meher Baba reminds us, it is not for the faint-hearted and the weak.

Lately, I have experienced the loss of control as being at the mercy, sometimes tender and sometimes rough, of the Masterful One. He sees beyond my smallest wishes for self-preservation, and is one hundred percent willing to wield his knife, usually without anesthesia, to make me bleed, all in the service of my highest destiny. Accepting that reality requires the greatest surrender possible. That surrender is one that I wrestle with now, and realize that surrender is not a final state (other than the great surrender at the end of our reincarnations); rather, it is a process to engage with each day. It is never about succeeding or failing because that construct comes from the ego and its tendency to evaluate and judge nearly everything. It is a matter of finding the compassionate part of who I am, and listening to the pain, the anguish, and the dark thoughts, welcoming all of them as part of the largest landscape ever, the one that takes me to His door, to an opening far more beautiful than anything I can imagine, as I relinquish control, and say yes to the Masterful One. In my saying yes, and finding kindness for myself as I struggle, I feel my worthiness, at last!

When I calculate how many times my heart has broken open, I realize that each time is yet another opportunity to feel the pain, to listen to its voice, to love it, and to hold it as a path to finding my gold, to embracing love. A Rumi poem describes this attitude aptly. He likens the Self to a guest house with many unexpected visitors, some of whom are not exactly welcome because they are difficult to tolerate. He suggests that these unexpected guests should all be welcomed, since perhaps their presence is functioning as a guide from beyond, helping me to wake up, and to fulfill Baba's mission, which was not to teach but to awaken.

What Does Surrender Mean to You?

By Alan Manoukian

When Laurent asked me, "What does surrender mean to you?" I found my mind went blank. All my concepts and interpretations in that moment felt empty, dishonest, and all I could say was, "I'll have to think about that". It seemed a difficult question to answer. Little did I know that soon after he posed this question the world would be overtaken by the largest pandemic since the Spanish Flu of 1918.

I'm currently in self quarantine with my wife Adrienne at our home due to California's mandatory shutdown from COVID-19. As you can imagine, I've had all kinds of thoughts and time to reflect on surrender since this started a week ago. The only thing that truly gives me some relief from all the fear and paranoia is actively surrendering my everything to Meher Baba as often as possible. Sometimes this even looks like sitting in our attic in total darkness and consciously dropping everything; mind, energy, and body into Baba's lap. Yet, it is not so easy as it sounds.

Often, my mind slips into negative thoughts and imagination. There are moments (especially after listening to the news) when massive, icy waves of fear seem to swallow me whole. I feel so far away from Baba and any inkling of love is drowned by another crash of painful resistance to accepting what is happening. In those times, I think of Baba and say His name but the words feel empty. I look at his photos and just can't connect. I feel my Father has gone from me and an experience of deep desolation and loneliness paints my mind-scape.

However, regardless of how terrifying a place my mind becomes, I know these moments are precious opportunities to witness the false sense of security which has kept me from surrendering in a deeper way to Baba. When faced with absolute uncertainty and possible harm or even death, my faith wavers because there is the reality that I'm at high risk for getting very ill from this disease since I have asthma. Baba's compassion is showing me that I must face all this doubt and negativity that was there all along.

Baba says,

> "I bring out your weaknesses because I love you. Be honest. Weaknesses there are. Do not be afraid of them...Who does not get bad thoughts? They are the foundation of life. No house can stand without its foundation. Thoughts can be good or bad, one should take care of one's action. Had it not been for the weaknesses of everyone, there would have been no difference between Me and you." [1]

It helps me when Baba says that bad thoughts are in the foundation of life. Baba is stressing the importance of being vigilant about how I behave regardless of my thoughts and feelings. I am standing on the foundation of lifetimes of sanskaras and it is inevitable that I will at times be overcome by the strong currents of my mind. The force of these negative thoughts lead me to seek His darshan. It's a requirement of the spiritual path to be beaten by the devastating blows of Maya. I must rely on Him to take care of everything, especially when my world falls apart.

Baba continues on this point when he says, [2]

> "...increasing surrender to the guidance of the master involves drastic curtailment of deceptive imagination–the roots of which are deeply embedded in the mental and emotional past of the pilgrim."

In a way, we are built to fail again and again in our efforts to remember and surrender to Him, especially through all the incredible hardships we must face. Baba goes on to say, [3]

> "In the end, all imagination comes to a standstill and is replaced by the true everlasting realization of God as the sole reality."

Ultimately, we are all on the long journey of falling into His arms.

When I first became a Baba lover, I had a question that no one around me could answer: "Why do atrocities and terrible things happen to people?" My mother's side of my family comes from the Armenian genocide and the Lebanese civil war. My father's side endured the genocide of indigenous people in Mexico and my grandfather was murdered when my dad was just a boy. Many years of seeking relief from the trauma and inherited grief left me feeling quietly resentful at God. Day after day as I looked at photos of Baba I would ask this question without receiving an answer. I was often overcome by hatred, rage, and resentment at all the injustice in the world. Sometimes I yelled at Him aloud, weeping and begging for relief. Then one night I had a dream. Baba is a boy playing and carefree. Suddenly I am yelling and demanding answers from young Merwan about all the unfairness and suffering in life. He stops in place and looks at me with an inquisitive, sad expression. Blinded by the wrath of my lifetimes of suffering, I continue screaming at Him for answers. Baba slowly ages into His teens, young adult, middle age, and elderly years. As I'm screaming for answers my heart is searing in tortuous pain. Then Baba reaches a certain elderly age and puts His hand out in a way to say "Stop." My whole body freezes in place, and He lifts His hand to His face in the gesture of "Be silent." Baba's eyes pierce into mine.

His wordless expression is an authoritative declaration that instantly dissolves all the struggle in my heart. The gravity of His compassion and forgiveness was undeniable proof of His Divinity. With just a glance, He wiped away so much. After waking from that dream, my mental gymnastics and torment of why terrible things happen in the world is no longer here. I realized in that moment with Baba what I was ultimately struggling with was the resistance to surrender what I can never understand until I am one with Him. It was a moment of surrendering all these seemingly permanent emotions and perceptions to God and ultimately an experience of faith in Him. In the same way when all these surging feelings of fear come over me during this global pandemic, I do my best to remember this is beyond my understanding and to do as He says by focusing more on loving Him than questioning Him. Moment to moment I must surrender that which is beyond my capacity.

Bringing it back to Laurent's question, "What does surrender mean to you?" Surrendering to Meher Baba is the most important work of my lifetime. Surrender means doing the work of offering everything to Him without questioning so much, even though I will fail again and again. To remember Him is not to remember some idea of long ago, but to meet God in the Eternal Present. He ever was, is, and will ever be. I live my everyday life with all the negative thoughts and doubts, joys and celebrations, but in any moment - there He is. Even through a pandemic and beyond my present form, there He is, gently dissolving this drop soul slowly but surely into the Infinite. How beautiful it is to know that no matter what happens, everything is a movement toward our Beloved.

Baba

By Cyprus Weichberger

Who do you believe in
Role models and gods, or heroes and stars
We all leave a footprint on Earth
It's about whether or not you're choosing to march
Oh Parvardigar
Monks and the Hindus, Christians, Islam
Buddha and Baba
With a cross and a heart
Where's the flames in the dark
Brazil and Umbanda
All of the possibilities that I ponder
God is relentless
Oh man, I feel the karma God father
consequences
Give me the ability to wonder
But still never know
Give us the burden of stutter
And the ideas to be trapped down under
Give us the ability to love
But never find your lover
Balance it out, all of the people we are judging
Reality is a dream, will I wake up to life?
Where will I go when I die?
My perception is blind
Where's paradise?

'Cause if all the wise want to do when they find
all of the truth behind our life
is leave all that they know behind
what will I have to do to get there and what is the price?
And how much better is the light?
Is our illusion the definition of Hell,
then how is the oblivion different?
The scribes figured it out
What happened to lies?
Also what happens to science?
Reincarnation is blowing my mind
We will do it again and again for a million times
rolling the dice on luck
and what our life will be like
And the fact that nothing gets faker than time
Just an illusion like everything else
Well karma is balance and balance divine
Suffer and suffer and suffer, wait why?
Want to go to heaven, but heavens too high
Who is locking the gates in the sky?
Still teaching myself how to try
We are all one
So if I am am being kind
Then I am being kind to myself
And there is no one else
Leave. the ego. on a shelf
It's not about the cards you've been dealt
You are the deck while eternity fell
Cheating is a joke there's no reason to tell
Everyone knows it's anxiety's smell
When you lock someone up, you put yourself in a cell
When you say that you love me, your words parallelled

That is the past so
Baba will help
Yeah Baba will help
In the times of need
You will sit there and pray ability to breathe
Change yourself, while you turn a new leaf
Pray to be all you can be
And pray to Baba
the Preserver and Protector of all we believe
no Beginning, no End, infinity
beyond comparison the one who can teach
No colour, no form, and without feats.
You are unlimited and unfathomable, the God who takes lead
beyond imagination, eternally bleak
Indivisible; only divine could see
Past present and future, and you always will be;
You are everywhere, You are in everything;
and ironically you are the keys to the prison that will set people free
You are in the opposite of all and yet related to everything
You are in and beyond all of the worlds, and all of the
distance you keep
You are imperceptible and in harmony
You are the knower of minds and heart, the emotion that we bleed
You are the beginning and end of all of my dreams
You are Knowledge itself and the wisdom we speak
Life and death the emotion of creed
You are the universe so wake us up from our sleep.

Surrendering

By Sarah Weichberger

When I think of the term surrender, I think of letting go of all human desire to control and allowing events to unfold as they may. This is not to say that I just sit back and let life take over, but instead I hope to observe and see that events happen as they do for a reason, and that we, as humans, are not always in charge. I do think that we can't always see the reason right away, and it can take time, and a retrospective view, to understand why events may have happened the way they did. Another important aspect for me is to not have attachment to outcomes. With this idea is also the letting go of wanting to control what other people do, or being angered by it. I still struggle with road rage in a big way. For me, letting go of anger can be tough. I often feel a sense of needing justice in a situation, and I feel that when things happen in a way that doesn't seem fair, I get upset. This would apply to my personal experiences, as well as things like hearing that a billionaire businessman earned thirteen billion dollars profit in one day. I see that in the news and I think, wow, he could end global hunger in one fell swoop, by helping the poor, but of course, he is not doing that. In the end, it is not my place to expect anything from others, yet it can be a source of frustration to me.

In my life I have seen my fair share of tragedy and personal loss. When my father committed suicide in 1985, when I was twenty, I carried that grief around for many years, and I believe that in doing so I myself became a victim, and was not able to move forward in my life. My creativity was stifled, and my belief in myself was injured by his actions. I felt that he had left me behind and that he had given up on me. Of course, nobody knows what causes someone to take their own life, and it certainly is not usually about anyone but that person. The reason I mention this is because for so many years, I felt the weight of that grief, and I wanted to understand why he had done that. Now, thirty-five years later, I see that all of the things we experience in this lifetime are there to teach us something, if only to teach us that we don't need to know why. Perhaps we just need to surrender to the chaos of the outer world, by understanding that there are always going to be aspects of life and the human condition that are part of the overall plan. Poverty, war, racism, classism, are all part of the human experience and will likely always exist.

For me, surrender means to let things be. To experience life, to have adventures, to love, to grieve, and to see that everything that we encounter in life is how it was meant to be for us. Yes, we play a part, by the decisions we make and the behavior we chose to embrace in any given situation, but in the end, what will be will be. That is a difficult place to get to. I certainly was not there at twenty, or thirty, or even forty years old. I tend to overthink things, and intellectualize things, in order to better understand "why?" This can be a very energy and time consuming practice, and even an avoidance tactic. It's like being a mouse on a wheel, exhausting and yet going nowhere. Now, my goal is to surrender to the "what is," without hoping to get to the bottom of it. I am still a work in progress.

I spent five months in India in 2009, staying at the Meher Baba center in Meherabad. During that time I had a profound realization that in life we are really living in a day by day existence. All we have is now. We can make plans, and have ideas of what we would like to do, where we would like to live, how much money we need, desiring material comforts, but really, at the end of the day, what matters most is that we have a place to sleep and people that we love in our lives, if we are so fortunate. Or we are alone, and that is also its own path. I saw so much poverty in India and yet the people were much happier than many I know and have seen in the west. They had next to nothing and shared what they had freely and lovingly. It seemed as though they had surrendered to their situation and because of this they were very gracious and kind and loving to each other, and to me, a total stranger. They were not spending their days lamenting what they did not have.

It took me so long to sit down and write this because I honestly don't know if I know what it means to surrender. I wanted to write about it, so here I am.

Do I know the true meaning of surrender?
Is it surrender to a master?
Surrender to the universe, allowing whatever happens to happen without any resistance?
Perhaps it is called acceptance?

I hope to achieve a balance within myself so that I am not so affected by what transpires in the world around me. Inner balance to me means to be able to live within the world and see all events as necessary, even when I can't make total sense of it. I have slowly begun to allow myself to let go, to flow with what is.

I am surrendering.

یار نماند آنکه با یار بساخت   بی

بساخت با خریدارهنکآ مفلس نشد

مید رن گرفت، کز شب نز آمه نور ا

بساختر که با خا ن یافتز آی اوگل ب

The one who conforms to the Friend will never be left friendless,
And the one who conforms to the customer will never be bankrupt.
The moon obtains light when not frightened away
by the darkness of the night,
The rose acquires fragrance when it gets used to the thorn.

Jalal-u-Din Rumi

Surrender and Interfaith Verbal Unity in Meher Baba's Message "The Highest of the High"

By Thomas Wolfe

These days when, as Rumi sings, the darkness of the night is frightening, and every day seems to hold a new thorn, it is imperative we hold closely to Meher Baba's call to Surrender. Issued in 1953, His message *"The Highest of the High"* holds some true gems shining bright that tell in the Beloved's own silent words what His wish is for our Surrender.

Also shared are scriptural examples of Baba's call to Surrender from Eight Faiths which to my heart and mind show clearly that the Avatar's call to Surrender has been consistent for 6,000 years from Zarathustra to Meher Baba.

Let us review two things Baba says in *"The Highest of the High"* about Surrender. First, after directly saying what He is *not* for, Baba says

> "I am for the few who, scattered amongst the crowd, silently and unostentatiously surrender their all–body, mind, and possessions— to Me. I am still more for those who, after surrendering their all, never give another thought to their Surrender."

Secondly, Baba says that it is possible to Surrender in a way to please him using the example

> "There are about 220 men and women from the East and the West who have so completely and utterly surrendered to Me that they would do anything I say. To Surrender is higher than to love, and

paradoxical as it may seem, to love me as I ought to be loved is impossible, yet to obey me is possible. Therefore to say you love me and yet not to obey me would be hypocritical".

So, Baba is for those who Surrender, Surrender is more attainable than love, and Thanks Be to God it is possible.

The scriptural examples of Baba's clarion call to Surrender come from Eight Faith traditions and are part of a larger compilation done of thirty-three common principles. Meher Baba of course, Zarathustra, Krishna, Buddha, The Tanakh (The Jewish scriptures), The Gospels of Jesus, Hazrat Muhammad, and the Quakers. Baba's two principles on Surrender that frame the examples are taken from *"The Seven Realities'* and *"12 Ways of Realizing Me"*. My prayer is that you will find, as I have, conviction that God's message has been consistent about Surrender for 6,000 years. The scriptural examples are presented without commentary as the Avatar's words on Surrender speak for themselves.

7 of 33: from *"The Seven Realities"*

"The only Real Surrender is that in which poise is undisturbed by any adverse circumstance, and the individual, amidst every kind of hardship, is resigned with perfect calm to the will of God."

Meher Baba:

"Wanting is a state of disturbed equilibrium of mind, and nonwanting is a state of stable poise. The poise of nonwanting can only be maintained by an unceasing disentanglement from all stimuli –whether pleasant or painful, agreeable or disagreeable. In order to remain unmoved by the joys and sorrows of this world, the mind must be completely detached from the external and internal stimuli." [1]

Zarathustra:

"O Wise Follower of God, I have taught
That action, not inaction, higher stands,
Obeying, then, His Will, worship through deeds.
The Great Lord, wondrous Guardian of the Worlds,
Through His Eternal Law discriminates,
Who are the truly Wise and who Unwise." [2]

Krishna:

"Surrendering all thoughts of outcome,
unperturbed, self-reliant,
he does nothing at all, even
when fully engaged in actions." [3]

"The resolute in yoga surrender
results, and gain perfect peace;
the irresolute, attached to results,
are bound by everything they do." [4]

Tanakh:

"When you pass through water,
I will be with you;
Through streams,
They shall not overwhelm you.
When you walk through fire,
You shall not be scorched;
Through flame,
It shall not burn you.
For I the Lord am your God,
The Holy One of Israel, your Savior." [5]

Buddha:

"Good people walk on, whatever befall; the good do not prattle, longing for pleasure; whether touched by happiness or sorrow, wise people never appear elated or depressed." [6]

Jesus:

"Not every one that saith unto me, Lord, Lord, shall enter into the kingdom of heaven; but he that doeth the will of my Father which is in heaven." [7]

Muhammad's Revelation:

"O you who have attained to faith! Seek aid in steadfast patience and prayer: for, behold, God is with those who are patient in adversity... And most certainly shall We try you by means of danger, and hunger, and loss of worldly goods, of lives and of [labour"s] fruits. But give glad tidings unto those who are patient in adversity – who, when calamity befalls them, say, 'Verily, unto God do we belong and, verily, unto Him we shall return.'" [8]

"Hence, we shall certainly bear with patience whatever hurt you may do us: for, all who have trust [in His existence] must place their trust in God [alone]!" [9]

Quakers:

"This people [Quakers] insists that Christianity teaches people to beat their swords into plowshares and their spears into pruning hooks and never again to train for war. They not only refused to take revenge for injuries received, condemning it as unchristian, but they freely forgave those who had been cruel to them–even when vengeance was within their power. Many notable examples of their efforts to overcome injustice and oppression could be provided." [10]

32 of 33: Surrenderance from "*12 Ways of Realizing Me:*"

"If your Surrenderance to Me is as wholehearted as that of one who, suffering from insomnia, surrenders to sudden sleep without fear of being lost, then you will have Me."

Meher Baba:

"Complete self-surrender and unquestioning love become possible when the disciple achieves unswerving faith in the Master." [11]

"Spiritual advancement is a succession of one surrender after another until the goal of the final surrenderance of the separate ego-life is completely achieved.... Therefore, in a sense, the most complete surrender to the Master is equivalent to the attainment of the Truth, which is the ultimate goal of all spiritual advancement." [12]

Zarathushtra:

"But, God, he who through the urge of heart,
Through sacrifice of Self, doth link himself,
And his own Inner Self with Love,
Finds Wisdom, and Knowledge's Wisdom, too;
Sheltered by Righteousness, he shall dwell with Them." [13]

Krishna:

"Surrendering all thoughts of outcome,
unperturbed, self-reliant,
he does nothing at all, even
when fully engaged in actions." [14]

"Those who realize the essence
of duty, who trust me completely
and surrender their lives to me –
I love them with very great love." [15]

Tanakh:

"Now do not be stiff necked like your fathers; submit yourselves to the Lord and come to His sanctuary, which He consecrated forever, and serve the Lord your God ... for the Lord your God is gracious and merciful; He will not turn His face from you if you return to Him." [16]

Buddha:

"His thought is quiet, quiet are his words and deed, when he has obtained freedom by true knowledge, when he has thus become a quiet man." [17]

Jesus:

"Not every one that saith unto me, Lord, Lord, shall enter into the kingdom of heaven; but he that doeth the will of my Father which is in heaven." [18]

Muhammad's Revelation:

"Yea, indeed: everyone who surrenders his whole being unto God, and is a doer of good withal, shall have his reward with his Sustainer; and all such need have no fear, and neither shall they grieve." [19]

"Behold the only [true] religion in the sight of God is [man"s] self-surrender unto Him;...Thus, [O Prophet,] if they argue with thee, say, "I have surrendered my whole being unto God, and [so have] all who follow me!" – and ask those who have been vouchsafed revelation aforetime, as well as all unlettered people, "Have you [too] surrendered yourself unto Him?" And if they surrender themselves unto Him, they are on the right path." [20]

Quakers:

> "I remembered that thou art omnipotent, that I had called thee Father, and I felt that I loved thee, and was made quiet in thy will, and I waited for deliverance from thee; thou hadst pity upon me when no man could help me; I saw that meekness under suffering was shown to us in the most affecting example of thy Son, and thou taught me to follow him, and I said, 'Thy will, O Father be done.'" [21]

Friends, it is time to end this short journey in celebration of God's consistent call over six thousand years to Surrender. Beloved Meher, of course, silently "says' it best, calling us to Surrender to His Unity in "a creative synthesis of ancient heritage":

> "The future of humanity is in the hands of those who have this Vision [of Universal Brotherhood], and the role of the East in that future will be an irreplaceable one if it knits its spiritual and human resources together into a creative synthesis of ancient heritage." - Meher Baba [22]

To end from the *"Highest of the High,"* is a directive from Baba that personally speaks to my heart and keeps me focused on this "Beads on One String" interfaith work as best I can, done with heart in Surrender to Him. My heart has found, even in flawed Surrender, as quoted from the quatrain of Rumi in the very beginning: "The one who conforms to the Friend will never be left friendless."

> "From time eternal, gods have been performing my real puja. What I want from all my lovers is real unadulterated Love, and from my genuine workers, I expect real work done" - Meher Baba [23]

We are All in the Same Boat: Obedience Then and Now

By Daniel J. Stone

Like many of those who came to Baba after He left His physical form, from the beginning I was faced with a core question–what does obedience to Baba mean now that He has physically departed? Sitting in Mandali Hall at Meherazad with Eruch Jessawalla and other mandali over the years, I found that many other pilgrims of my era also shared this question.

We know that Baba emphasized obedience as a sine qua non of the spiritual life–without it, the spiritual life is not possible. He said,

> "Understanding has no meaning. Love has meaning. Obedience has more meaning. Holding my daaman has most meaning." [1]

He thereby placed obedience as second in importance, only next to maintaining one's connection with Him at all costs.

Now, in an era when the last of Baba's close mandali members are no longer with us, at least three generations of Baba-lovers coexist in today's world:

<u>Generation One:</u>	Those who physically met Baba
<u>Generation Two:</u>	Those who met and were influenced directly by the mandali
<u>Generation Three:</u>	Those who had little or no contact with the mandali

Having grown up as a Baba-lover who was fortunate to meet and spend time with many of the mandali over a number of years, I belong to that second generation. The time I spent with them was instrumental in orienting myself in my "new life" as a Baba-lover. Among the many treasured benefits I received was learning something about Baba's ways – what He expects of His lovers, and what He offers us in our efforts to come closer to Him. The mandali and other close lovers recounted story after story on the importance of obedience, and the lengths Baba went to help them cultivate this most necessary attribute for those who aspire to love Him as He would want us to love Him.

Given the importance that Baba places on obedience, I have frequently reflected on its meaning, and on how to practice it in my life with Baba. The mandali and other Baba-lovers have imparted many experiences and lessons on this theme. Coupled with Baba's explanations and my own personal experiences, they have helped me better understand the levels of obedience an individual can practice as they follow Baba. Some of Baba's most central prayers also contain wisdom for understanding what obedience means in the context of following His wish. Additionally, a Sufi concept about the layers of the heart has guided me in developing a personal practice for listening to inner guidance that fulfills Baba's wishes. I have also contemplated the roles that obstacles, failure, forgiveness, and surrender play as an individual pursues a life of obedience to Baba. But ultimately, I have considered how the concept of obedience to Meher Baba is as relevant today as it was to those who were with Him physically. I cover all these elements in this chapter, which taken together reflects the way I have synthesized what I have garnered over the years about obedience.

Learning about Baba's ways is a lifelong process that draws from many sources. And so through these various avenues I have come to understand that practicing obedience is central in all pursuits. In a nutshell, I have learned that practicing obedience means learning to listen to Baba speaking in our hearts, at all times and under all conditions; doing our best to carry out the wishes from Him that we receive therein; and surrendering to Him, as the fruits of our efforts continue to unfold in our lives.

So now let us consider what obedience meant "then", at a time when the mandali were trained and utilized by Baba for His work; following which we will consider what obedience means "now", as we are find ourselves in a different era as regards the availability of Baba's guidance and direction.

Obedience Then

Tirelessly and generously, the mandali shared their treasure chest of stories of their times with Baba, as well as their own reflections on discipleship with Him. Through these stories, they imparted many gems about how to hold fast to His daaman throughout their extraordinarily demanding lives of service to the Avatar. They also shared their reflections about what they feel is required for us to strengthen our connection to Baba, in this time when the Avatar is no longer physically present.

In Mandali Hall at Meherazad, one of the questions most frequently asked of Baba's close mandali member, Eruch Jessawalla was, "How can we obey Him now that He is no longer available in the body to give us direct orders?" I never heard Eruch pull rank as a mandali member or Baba-lover, and in that vein he would sometimes respond by saying, *"Brother, we are now all in the same boat; we all know what would please Him."* In other words, whether you were with Him physically or not, the task of a Baba-lover is the same for all – to find a reliable foundation for our lives with Him through inner connection. Never do I recall any of the mandali suggesting that the challenge that we newer Baba-lovers were facing is essentially different from the challenges that they too faced after Baba dropped His physical form.

Now, those times of friendship and connection with the mandali are no longer available. And those who had that mandali experience are left with whatever they gained from associating with them in their youth. But if Eruch's words are true, each Baba-lover, regardless of whether they are mandali, spent time with mandali, or never knew mandali, are *"...all in the same boat."* That is: Baba remains directly available for inner connection and guidance, just as He did during His physical lifetime, and just as He did during the "mandali period" – that time after He dropped His body when so many of His mandali were available to the newcomers. All are left with the same challenge – how to grow closer and closer to Baba.

Baba often emphasized the importance of getting closer to Him, and stressed that the challenge of doing so will only continue to intensify. As He shared in one particularly apt metaphor, as the "umbrella spins faster and faster" – and He has assured us that it will – we must become so close to the center of the umbrella that no amount of spinning will allow us to be thrown off. [2]

As Baba emphasized repeatedly throughout the entire course of His Advent – and as His mandali also emphasized – obedience is the watchword for following a Master. It is the means by which we come to the center of the umbrella, instead of getting thrown off. Countless mandali stories emphasize the importance of obedience, and how disobedience of His orders was not only a source of displeasure for Baba, but could have other adverse consequences also.

One well known example concerns Adi K. Irani, Baba's secretary and one of His longest-term and closest mandali. On one occasion, Adi was given the order by Baba to drive somewhere in Ahmednagar along with his brother Rustom to do an errand for Baba, and to return by noon. Baba was very particular about needing to be back by noon. However, Adi neglected to attend sufficiently to the time, and was late in returning. In the process, he accidentally ran over a child, who died from the injuries. [3]

The threat of jail timc hung over his head for a long time, though fortunately the court case was eventually dropped, perhaps through Baba's divine intervention. This incident demonstrates how serious Baba's orders were, and how followers of Baba can even risk losing an aura of protection when they do not properly follow them.

Another example on the importance of obedience comes from Kitty Davy, who was the housekeeper for the ashram at Panchgani in 1941. [4]

Baba had gone away for His work, and left Kitty in charge of providing tea and bread, with the proviso that no one was to get toast. As it turned out, while Baba was away some of the ashram-ites complained to Kitty about not liking the soggy plain bread, and asked Kitty if they might have hot buttered toast. Out of compassion, Kitty made an exception to the rule. As others saw this happen, more requested and were given dispensation to have their toast, to the point that by the time Baba returned, He found that half the group was enjoying toast. Baba took Kitty severely to task for having neglected His orders, saying to the assemblage, "Kitty cares more about pleasing others than pleasing me." Kitty, who felt she had been acting out of love, became so exasperated with Baba for saying this that she ended up throwing an orange at Him (which fortunately fell short of its target). Baba then relieved her of her housekeeper responsibility at that time, and said, "Now we will start with a clean slate." So, while He was forgiving, there were still consequences to her lapse. This incident seemed to deepen Kitty's understanding of the importance of obedience – an understanding that she conveyed to so many of those that she met, befriended, and counseled during her years of service to Baba at the Meher Center in Myrtle Beach.

These are examples from when Baba was physically present. I can also find examples from my own life where I have felt an order from Baba that I did not pay attention to, and then suffered the consequences. Fortunately there are also times when I feel I have followed what felt like an order from Baba – even when it was difficult – and felt His pleasure in my obedience. So it seems that pleasing Baba today through obedience remains as important as it was during the period when He was with us physically.

Types of Obedience

Baba specifies two different kinds of obedience – intellectual and literal. [5]

In intellectual obedience, the obedience is primarily based on the person's intellectual understanding of the Master and His orders.

> "When you are intellectually convinced about the greatness and perfection of the Master, you have love and respect for him but are unable to follow his orders literally. Reason being the basis of your conviction, you find it difficult to divorce it from your understanding of the Master and his orders."

Baba goes on to compare intellectual obedience to literal obedience.

> "Through intellectual obedience to the Master, you can annihilate all your sanskaras... [however] the result comes much quicker if your obedience is literal... which prepares [the aspirant] to follow the Master's orders implicitly – irrespective of their satisfying his critical spirit. Such literal obedience is not even bound by the requirement that the real significance of the orders should be within the intellectual comprehension of the pupil, and it is the best type of obedience to which you can aspire."

Given this, intellectual obedience might be considered explicit obedience which is filtered through the aspirant's intellectual understanding of what is being asked of him/her. Literal obedience - following the Master's orders implicitly - on the other hand involves committing to carrying out that guidance, *even when the intellectual mind rebels against it.* It also involves "reading" the Master as to what would please Him, even if not stated explicitly. This implicit level of literal obedience requires a deep listening for inner guidance from Baba, and while both forms of obedience are important, the literal obedience, which includes this implicit obedience, is the "faster" form. Overall, the essence of learning obedience seems to be about learning to make every effort to please the Beloved, in not only our actions but also our thoughts.

For the vast majority of His lovers during Baba's physical lifetime, Baba occasionally gave explicit orders, providing them the opportunity to practice intellectual obedience. For example, there were times when people were asked to keep silence for a period of time, or to say the Master's Prayer and Repentance Prayer daily. Sometimes a select group of lovers would be called to Baba, where He asked them to obey certain instructions such as observing periods of celibacy. And then there were those times that Baba gave some of His lovers the opportunity to accept orders from Him, without actually requiring that they do so. Perhaps one of the best-known examples of this was during the preparation for the New Life when He called a number of His lovers to Him and gave them the choice to either pursue the New Life under the conditions He explained, or pursue it under amended conditions. [6]

Actually, in the early years Baba was known to extract agreements from His mandali and lovers so often that He was affectionately known to some as the "Agreement-Walla." Some of these agreements were actually executed through written documents. One such set of documents asked people to indicate whether they would give their property, money or life to Baba, and this required their signature.

CIRCULAR LETTER No. 3

Date........................

Dear Baba,

As explained to me personally by Eruch and Pendu, I agree, on my own free will and responsibility, to obey you unconditionally by dedicating to you any one, or more or all of the 'following,'—entirely in the interest of spiritual life.:—

1. MY MONEY — YES / NO ....

2. MY PROPERTY — YES / NO ....

3. MY SERVICE — YES / NO ....

4. MY VERY LIFE — YES / NO ....

My Remarks on the above (if any).

....

....

....

....

....

....

....

Yours devotedly

....

MY NAME & ADDRESS
(In Block Letters)

....

....

....

....

Children and teenagers were not exempted from the opportunity to learn the life of obedience to Him. Baba's sister Mani tells of having been given "little orders' by Baba when she was a child,

> "She must do her lessons, write to Baba once a week, listen to Mother, and not run away from home to be with Him." [7]

By the time she was eleven, Mani says that she was old enough for "big orders' which mainly had to do with leading a pure life at all times and in all circumstances.

Naosherwan Anzar shares that when in his teens, he was determined that if Baba did not grant his wish to come join the mandali, he would disobey Him by settling down in a field next to Meherabad. In a response to Naosherwan's declaration, Baba wrote him,

> "To obey the God Man is the highest form of worship to God in human form; obey me implicitly if one day you want to know me as I am." [8]

Yet other stories illustrate the distinction between intellectual obedience and literal, (or implicit) obedience, and highlight Baba's emphasis on the latter. Bhau Kalchuri shares one such instance that occurred when Baba was with Gustadji in Mandali Hall as He gave Bhau the responsibility to write a letter. Soon after Bhau left the hall to begin his work, Baba called him back into the hall to fetch Gustadji a glass of water. Bhau did this, and then returned to his room to resume the writing task, only to be called by Baba again to clean up some crumbs from under Gustadji's plate. While Bhau was removing these crumbs, Baba asked about Bhau's progress on the letter. At this point, Bhau's irritation broke through, and he complained to Baba that here Gustadji was doing nothing, while he (Bhau) was trying to complete the assignment that Baba had given him. Baba then got severe with Bhau, saying that Gustadji knew what Baba wanted and was doing it, and was therefore pleasing Him. However, even though he was doing the work assigned, Bhau's obedience was not pleasing Him.

This story seems to indicate that Gustadji was practicing "literal obedience," inferring what Baba wanted and following that. Bhau, on the other hand, may have intellectually been following Baba's directive, but had not followed his Master's orders implicitly; he even rebelled against the continual interruptions because they didn't satisfy Bhau's critical spirit as to what should have constituted reasonable obedience. However, essentially Baba wanted Bhau to practice literal, or implicit, obedience. Therefore, obedience is about something more subtle than simply following orders – it is about our ability to intuit what Baba would want of us – both in action and attitude – and follow that intuition, thereby pleasing Him.

Another example of "reading" what Baba wanted and following that occurred during the New Life. At one point Baba's companions were offered the choice of staying with Him or venturing off on their own. Dr. Donkin chose to proceed on the New Life on His own, because he felt it was what Baba wanted from him. Thus, he was following not a direct order, but the dictates of his own "reading" of what would please Baba. [9]

Earlier on in His physical manifestation, Baba would often meet His lovers and provide them guidance about career, family, finances, and other such facets of human life. In the later years however, Baba seemed to offer less and less of this kind of explicit direction. For example, when one young man asked Baba what profession to pursue, Baba asked him what he was considering. When he said "psychology," Baba simply said to pursue that, and He would be there helping him. Perhaps this shift from giving explicit orders to redirecting people to following their intuition represented a general sense of maturation of His lovers. It seems that Baba began expecting them to internalize His help, to free them from waiting for His explicit guidance, so they could sensitize themselves to His inner guidance.

Even the mandali were not continually given a stream of orders from Baba, and had to learn to attune within to receive inner guidance from Him. Elizabeth Patterson and Norina Matchabelli, who together founded Baba's Center in Myrtle Beach, did have a great deal of communication with Him during the founding of the Center. But there were also periods when such communication was not possible and they were faced on a daily basis with countless decisions that could not wait for His response. Perhaps most importantly, they had been trained to listen for His inner guidance without fully expecting or relying on Him to tell them what to do. Interestingly, there was an incident during one of Baba's visits to Myrtle Beach when He was asked by one of the American group heads how they should organize and conduct their Baba meetings. Baba's response was *"why be limited by what I tell you?"* In other words, He has much greater scope to speak within us, rather than simply giving His lovers external direction.

After all, what was the meaning of His silence if not to prepare us – not just a few in the world, but eventually all of humanity – to listen and obey the inner voice, that Baba promised is His voice? So Baba over time seemed to be directing people more and more to rely on that inner voice rather than on the direct explicit orders that had so informed the training of His early mandali and disciples.

Obedience Now

The mandali would sometimes reassure us by saying how fortunate we all were to have come to love Him without having met Him physically, because we did not have to break the habit of dependency on Baba's direct orders. Instead, we could learn more direct inward communication with Baba. We now live in an unparalleled time in history where everyone can pursue a genuine and meaningful inner relationship with the Avatar, unhampered by any external conditions or requirements. And Baba has promised us that if we make the effort to establish and deepen that inner relationship, He will respond accordingly. A major way to pursue that relationship is through practicing implicit obedience. But what does this really entail?

Baba gave general guidance for living, such as not to partake of drugs, engage in promiscuous sexual relations, or get involved with other masters. However there is a huge scope of behavior beyond these areas that is not addressed in His published messages. While adherence to the guidance Baba provides through these messages is important, it is that larger scope of behavior that provides His lovers with prime opportunities to practice implicit obedience, thereby developing our intuitive reliance upon Him.

Baba said He came to raise the level of human functioning from "reason" to "intuition." Intuition is a primary means that allows us to discern what He wants of us and what would please Him. Exercising this reliance on intuition provides the opportunity to grow and mature in our relationship with Him. In the latter years before dropping His body He seemed to increasingly encourage His lovers to rely on this intuitive faculty. Learning this reliance seems all-the-more important today, now that He is no longer physically with us.

The Wish and Obedience

Baba made it clear that "the lover has to fulfill the wish of the Beloved." His beautiful exposition called "My Wish," highlights what the lover can do to fulfill Baba's wish. [10]

This message provides genuine guidance for those who aim to please Baba, which is of course the essence of obedience. To help His lovers, Baba has also given out three prayers that He encouraged lovers to say regularly: The Masters Prayer, Repentance Prayer, and Beloved God prayer. Many lovers take the daily repetition of these prayers as an implicit act of obedience to Baba, even though He didn't actually order their recitation.

There is, however, a very important nuance in one of the prayers that seems particularly relevant for those who are attempting to learn the practice of obedience. The final line of the Prayer of Repentance is generally translated as, *"Forgive me for my constant failure to think, speak, and act according to Your will."* Eruch used to remark that this translation of the prayer was a source of confusion. If everything that happens is Baba's will (for as He has said, *"not a leaf falls except if it is my will"*), how could one ever fail to think, speak, or act according to His will?

Eruch went on to say that the answer can be found in the way the prayer was translated from its original form in Gujerati. The word that Baba gave for "will" in Gujerati, "*marji*", actually can mean either "*wish*" or "*will.*" When translated into English, the word "will" was used, which Baba indicated was erroneous; however it was not corrected, so it has become memorialized in the prayer as "will." But Eruch indicated that a truer rendering of the prayer might have it conclude, *"Forgive me for my constant failures to speak, think, and act according to Your wish."*

Through this statement Baba has given us an important key to obedience. For it is now our task as lovers of Baba to find a way to increase our capacity to think, speak, and act as He would wish. By acting as He would wish, we inherently obey Him and please Him. All efforts to intuitively follow the guidance of Baba's voice within can be understood as efforts to obey Him. Conversely, our resistance to listening to that voice, or choosing not to follow its dictates can perhaps be seen as acts of non-obedience (or perhaps even "disobedience").

Inner Guidance and Obedience

Baba has said,

> "I am never silent. I speak eternally. The voice that is heard deep within the soul is My voice – the voice of inspiration, of intuition, of guidance. To those who are receptive to this voice, I speak." [11]

Baba's silence can be understood as one of, if not the primary, archetypal acts that He performed for the upliftment of humanity. When He breaks His silence, humanity as a whole will then be able to quiet the mind sufficiently enough to hear and rely on the inner voice from God as their trusted source of guidance for their lives. Having humanity as a whole reoriented to listening for the voice of God/Baba within – this is perhaps the change in consciousness that Baba said would happen when He broke His silence – something that has never happened before! In this way, people will learn to obey the voice of God as the foundation for their lives, a truly transformational shift for humanity.

For lovers of Meher Baba today, that shift has already begun, as we take the opportunity to continually exercise and expand our capacity to attune to this voice of guidance within. Baba said,

> "The book that I shall make people read is the book of the heart that holds the key to the mystery of life." [12]

Learning to listen to His voice within is essentially learning to read the book of the heart. How can we expand our ability to read this all-important *"book of the heart"*? To do this, it is first important to discern what inner voice we are actually listening to. One branch of Sufism describes four different layers of the heart. I find that this paradigm provides a helpful orientation to the process of finding inner guidance.

The first layer of the heart is sometimes referred to as the layer of the *nafs*. Nafs are impressions of the mind, so when we listen to this layer, we are listening to the thoughts – what we like, what we don't like, what we want, and what we don't want. This is sometimes referred to as the "monkey mind."

The second layer is associated with emotions that are triggered by our thoughts – anger, sadness, fear, and all their variations. However, emotions come and go, and are not particularly reliable as sources of guidance. Sometimes "trusting our gut" is a justification for simply acting upon our own desires. Baba described these emotions once as "feverish imagination working under the stimulus of desire." The drive at this layer is primarily to enhance pleasure and avoid pain.

The third layer of the heart is where we actually begin to be able to hear the voice of intuition. The word for heart in Arabic ["*qalb*"] actually means "that which turns", and in this layer we have turned our focus from our normal ego-ic orientation towards Baba so that we can begin to "hear" His voice. Of course, we do not "hear" only, or even primarily, through an audible medium. Often "hearing" comes through subtly sensing Baba's guidance through more subtle or refined feelings. It is not necessarily or even primarily associated with any words at all. Learning to listen at this third layer of the heart begins the development of our ability to "read the book of the heart."

The fourth layer of the heart ["*latif*"] is sometimes referred to as "the Secret." Here, consciousness is firmly established in hearing and responding to this inner voice on increasingly refined levels. And from this point there is no further turning back to the earlier layers. It is generally a layer that is inhabited by more advanced aspirants.

While this paradigm about the layers of the heart has its origin in Sufism, it maps almost exactly with what Baba has said:

> "When you feel something is intuitive and you have no doubt about it, then know it is real. Passing doubtful thoughts and temporary emotional feelings should not be given importance. But when you feel it touches your heart, follow it. When it is from the mind, it is not intuition. Intuition means that which comes from the heart. In the divine path, first there is intuition, then inspiration, then illumination, and finally Realization. If it touches your heart, follow it. And God willing from today you will know that if it is intuition it is right." [13]

In experimenting with these ideas over the years I have learned to begin by posing the question to Baba about that for which I am seeking guidance. Then, even before listening for the guidance, I commit to Baba that whatever guidance I receive – as clearly as I can discern it – I will follow it. Having done those two things, I am then prepared to open myself to listening for Baba's guidance on the question or challenge I am facing.

For those who are well established in the deeper layers of the heart, the process can actually be quite simple. Baba told Dina Tilati, one of His earliest and closest lovers, that all she needed to do to get His guidance was to put her hand over heart and ask Baba sincerely for help in whatever she was wanting. Then the very first thought that came to her should be taken as His guidance, and she was to follow it. And in no way was she to second guess it. However simple this may appear, it certainly seems to require that one is firmly established in that third layer of the heart.

There are no doubt other ways to access this inner guidance. However it is done, following this kind of inner guidance process requires placing full trust in Baba to guide us. This may seem a tall order, especially until we have developed the confidence that Baba's guidance is for our benefit. But over time and through experience, that trust will naturally grow as we come to recognize, as Hafiz has said, "*Whatever the master does is of the highest benefit to all concerned.*" [14]

And as our experience with this approach to life expands, our reliance on Baba also expands.

Risk-Taking and Reliance

Practicing obedience at this level of intimacy entails taking risks with Baba. By putting ourselves into His hands in this way, we accept that there is a source of guidance and control beyond what we may have habitually relied on through our more reasoned mind. But it seems that Baba actually encouraged people to take risks when it came to the spiritual life. A saying that has been attributed to Baba is *"in matters of health, we should take no risks; in matters of wealth we should take some risks; and in matters of God we should take every risk."* It is up to us to put ourselves in His hands, take the great risk of looking to Him for our guidance, and aligning our lives with that guidance.

A provocative statement, attributed to both Gurdjieff and Winston Churchill, says: *"Play with more than you can afford to lose to learn how to play the game."* I felt encouragement from the mandali to do just that – to be bold in experimenting with Baba by putting into His hands every decision that I face. This included decisions that seem very big and those that seem minor. In my own life, I have used this approach to present Baba with a range of questions – from ones with seeming import, regarding career and professional activities, marriage, family, and major purchases or commitments, to ones that appeared relatively trivial like whether to go out to a restaurant, whether to purchase a book, or what movie to go to. Through this, I have found it possible to develop a greater level of trust in receiving and acting upon the guidance I receive.

In the *Discourses* Baba said that in the spiritual life there should be no distinction between "big" and "small" – that all things are fodder for our care and attention and we should not create a hierarchy of importance among them. He encouraged us to turn to Him for all things in our life, treating Him both as father and mother. Turning to Him for guidance in everything big and small is a way to cultivate reliance upon Him. In Sufism, reliance is known as "*tawakkul*," or the reliance upon Allah, and is viewed as one of the most fundamental qualities a lover of God should develop. Bal Natu echoes this same sentiment in volumes of *Conversations with the Awakener*, in which he continually asks Baba to join him in facing all facets of his life – large and small.

And if we are looking to Him for guidance throughout our day for all things big and small, are we not coming closer to thinking, speaking, and acting according to His wish? We are, in other words, practicing deep obedience to Baba, developing our reliance on Him and, through these daily processes, growing our relationship with Him.

Barriers to Inner Guidance

We have now considered implicit obedience as a function of listening to and following inner guidance from Baba. But of course being able to do this may not always seem so simple. So what gets in the way of this kind of implicit obedience? There have been countless times in my life when I have failed to obey Baba – either by not seeking guidance, not hearing the guidance clearly, or not following the guidance I am given. In these experiences, I have found three primary barriers to listening to and receiving Baba's inner guidance.

1. I may not seek Baba's guidance often enough. There are many different times during each day when I could look to Him to guide me. Sometimes it is with relatively simple choices I am faced with and sometimes it is with more complex or far-reaching ones. Each, however, offers the opportunity to turn to Baba and ask "what would you have me do in this situation?" As such they are all opportunities to draw closer to Him, and to reduce the frequency of my "failure to think, speak, and act according to Your wish."

2. I may not be training myself to listen with discernment for His inner guidance. And this most often occurs when I am guided by my own desires or preconceptions. "Desires' are when I hold a preference for what I "want," while essentially going through the motions of asking for Baba's guidance and without actually being receptive to hearing Him. "Preconceptions' occur when I impose a "spiritually correct" answer to the question I am posing. Such "correct answers' are a product of my own mind, rather than allowing the guidance to arise from the heart. Instead of going deeper to find my own answer, this concept of what the "right" answer would be can easily supersede my own ability to discern the soft inner voice of intuition that Baba says is His voice.

As long as I am filtering my experience of Baba's guidance through either desires or preconceptions, I am immune to hearing His voice clearly. Primarily I have found that Baba's guidance comes through feeling rather than thoughts or words; so when I am searching for guidance, I am trying to be attentive to when desires or preconceptions present themselves, and then let them go and drop into a deeper part of my heart.

3. Finally, I may not be fully committed, when seeking guidance, to follow through with my commitment to follow the guidance I feel from Him. As noted earlier, a pre-condition for creating greater receptivity with Baba is to commit to following the guidance, even in advance of receiving it. This amounts to clearly putting my trust in Baba, as I am closing the loopholes that I might otherwise use to reject guidance that does not suit me. Once I receive that guidance–as clear or unclear as it may be–I am then committed to following it. However, on occasion I have asked for the guidance and then chosen to ignore it, as if it is only a "second opinion", to be considered on an equal par with my own preferences. When I do this, I seem to dull my capacity to continue hearing His "voice."

It is as if Baba has created through His silence a channel within each of us to have access to the voice of His guidance. These three barriers seem to have the impact of clogging up that channel. Our efforts to more frequently access this channel, and to use it wisely and with commitment, seem to help keep the channel open and deepen it.

Failure and Forgiveness

Learning obedience is a lifelong process, or more comprehensively, it is the work of many lifetimes. Learning is inevitably accompanied with failures, and there are plenty of examples in the lives of the mandali where they failed to obey Baba. It seemed that Baba was always ready to forgive those who failed to obey once the failure was recognized and there was sufficient repentance for it. Baba's forgiveness seemed to usually begin with the errant one acknowledging the failure to Baba without justification; and with a feeling of remorse and a determination to try and do better. Eruch once said, *"If you feel remorse for what you have done, Baba said that is a sign of His forgiveness."* Baba also counseled on avoiding excessive self-flagellation which has a demoralizing effect and is not conducive to the spiritual life. [15]

Arnavaz Dadachanji in Gift of God, p. 132, also addresses this question of the consequences of disobedience: *"Sometimes people say that because they didn't obey Baba, He has punished them by giving them suffering; but Baba never punishes... if we obey, we benefit; if we don't, then we go the way of destiny."* In this sense, we can perhaps better understand how Baba indicated that obedience is truly a gift from master to man.

While Baba often expressed His forgiveness directly in His physical lifetime, there is no reason to believe it is any less available in this post-mandali era. Perhaps it is even easier to gain His forgiveness for our errors, if they arise from a sincere effort to listen to and follow His guidance. The process of developing intuitive capabilities, after all, inherently requires risk-taking to learn what inner signals and guidance to trust.

It should also be noted that the outcome of obedience is not always the most apparently pleasant or positive outcome, and may even sometimes result in apparent ruination. Merwan Mistry tells a story about how as a young man, he used to be a formidable cricket player, able to consistently score points when he was at bat. Baba one time asked him if Merwan took Baba's name when he was at bat, to which he said "no". While not a direct order from Baba, Merwan took it as Baba's wish that he should do so, so he started taking Baba's name before he would bat. He found that once he started doing this, he was consistently put out each time. This did not deter him though, and from this experience he came to understand that the purpose of Baba's request was not to further his abilities as a cricketer, but to bring him closer to Baba. For Baba never promised that by following Him, a person would better fulfill their desires. The promise of obedience seems to be that through diligent practice, it draws us closer in His Love.

Obedience and Surrender

The exploration of obedience as the effort to follow Baba's voice within naturally moves to the question of surrender. In Meher Baba's "Seven Realities," He explains the final of the seven realities (and perhaps the ultimate) as

> "The only Real Surrender is that in which the poise is undisturbed by any adverse circumstances, and the individual, amidst every kind of hardship, is resigned with perfect calm to the will of God."

In this statement, the *"will of God"* is presented as that which ultimately sets the course for each of our life experiences. It is also understood to be that which is beyond the volitional power of the individual; i.e., the individual is not in a position to ultimately determine what that ultimate "will" is or to change it. Meher Baba has said that not a leaf falls except by His will, much as Jesus said, "all the hairs on your head have been numbered."

So we are left in the position of exercising our own "apparent will", as Baba made it clear that there is in fact no such thing as free will. This then leaves us with the conundrum of figuring out whether we should act as if we have free will, or to simply wait for God's will to show itself.
Baba responds to that conundrum as follows:

> "The truth of one's own perception and realization is the only road by which wholeness may be restored to the inner psychic being. In no other way can man obtain release from the chains that tie the limited ego-mind to the colossal cosmic illusion which hides from him the perennial spring of the Divinity within." [16]

In other words, for all of us who are still trapped in illusion, our own level of "perception and realization" would seem to indicate that we have free will. Therefore, according to what Baba has said, we must act as if we have free will, since that is what we experience as the reality. Simultaneously, however, Baba has told us that we must always keep in the back of our minds that everything happens only by His will, and that it is therefore determined by Him. In other words, we do not in fact have free will in reality, even though it appears to us as if we do.

If we are to act as if we have free will, then we can choose to act out of obedience to what we feel would please Baba, even though Baba has assured us that in reality such actions are also a function of His will. However, those acts of obedience to Baba would be actions that would ultimately free us from the illusion to which we are tied.

And that attitude of acting "as if" we have free will, through obedience, while at the same time accepting that whatever happens is by His will, leads us directly into the attitude of surrenderance. For surrender is that state we are in as we have accepted all that happens to be a function of His will. As Eruch had said, *"I exercise my free will to become His slave."* And today we are all in the position of exercising our apparent free will to become obedient to His wish, and thereby come closer and closer to Him in love and surrender.

Obedience Then and Now

So Baba's direct orders were prominent, especially in relationship to His mandali and other close ones during His lifetime. He also left general direct orders to His lovers through vehicles such as "*My Wish.*" However, it is also true that the mandali and other close lovers were trained and matured over time in their ability to read the "book of their hearts' to intuitively know what would please Baba, without direct explicit orders. In this way, they attuned themselves inwardly to Baba in a way that increasingly guided their lives over the years, into the years when He was no longer physically present to direct their lives. In this sense, when it comes to obeying Baba, their situation is truly no different from the situation of those members of Generation Two who sat in Mandali Hall and asked the mandali for guidance, or for Generation Three – those without either direct Baba or mandali contact in this current life.

Two other perspectives may be worth considering in exploring how requirements and opportunities in this new era might compare those available to earlier generations.

First, a newer generation of Baba lovers is emerging–one that had little or no contact with mandali. Based on several conversations I have had with lovers from that generation, I understand that they not only had little or no mandali contact, but also that many are also not necessarily focused on the mandali as a central source for discovering the core of their guidance about how to follow Baba.

The mandali told many of us in the Second Generation that we were fortunate to not have had physical contact with Baba, so somehow our following of Baba was in a sense "purer" by virtue of being solely inwardly guided. If this is the case, perhaps this Third Generation could be seen as that much more fortunate for not having contact with the mandali. For in that sense, they may be even more directly amenable to cultivate inner guidance with Baba without any undue influence from outside sources that might dilute that inner relationship. And if so, might this possibly yield an even purer form of discipleship? Perhaps a dialogue would be productive between those who were more schooled by the mandali and those without much if any connection to the mandali; for it seems clear that we have entered a new era in the Baba family, and much remains to be done to integrate our multi-generational Baba family.

One other possibility is also worth considering. Perhaps some or many of those Third Generation lovers are actually reincarnated souls who had been with Him in their last lifetime – even some might be mandali of His circle. In response to a question about what Baba meant when He said that those who take His name on breathing their last would "come to Him," Baba's sister Mani has been known to say that one of possibilities was being born in one's next life into a Baba family, thereby having the earliest opportunity to be connected to Baba. So while they may appear chronologically younger, they may well be souls with great spiritual backgrounds.

From this perspective, some or many of the current Third Generation of Baba-lovers may well have been close ones who had remembered Baba at the time of passing from their most recent past life. If so, then they potentially had the experience of having been trained by Baba through direct orders and the practice of obedience. And the learning that was accrued from those experiences would have been stored in their mental bodies, and would be accessible for them in their subsequent incarnations. So in a very literal sense, there may be no difference between the three generations of Baba lovers that were posited at the beginning of this chapter.

Both of these possibilities would seem to give even further support to those words from Eruch – words that continue to echo across the years since his passing in 2001 – that when it comes to finding the source from Baba for our obedience, *"We are all in the same boat."* In no way can we revert to believing that direction and guidance from Baba is limited to that which He gave only when He was in His physical form. We seem to be in the era when His full Avataric public manifestation is getting closer. And as it approaches, it seems that He has made His inner guidance increasingly available to each of His lovers, through expanding our capacity to listen to Him speaking in our hearts. And if we follow these dictates of the heart, He has blessed us with an unparalleled opportunity to come closer and closer to Him, through our obedience and surrender.

Surrender

By Dale Draeger

One of the important ways one can surrender is by accepting and growing as a person; developing who we are in this lifetime. Each one of us chose to be born with the goal of being excellent at being themselves. We came into this life to be the best Laurent, or Dale, or Harvey we could be.

What attributes, gifts, insights were you born with? How can you give to others using your abilities? To accept the gifts one has and to develop them is an act of surrender to the Truth within.

Of course it isn't easy. If this were an easy undertaking perhaps it wouldn't be worth the trip! There are and will be obstacles. Sometimes the adversity is dramatic enough to be worthy of a movie. There is always someone who is critical of who we are. Sometimes it is the family we are born into. Perhaps some of that criticism is helpful information and can send us on our way, bigger and stronger.

If the criticism is not helpful but is negative and draining, perhaps that person is someone to avoid. However, we can do ourselves a favor and speed up the process of being our best selves by looking at the difficult times with the intent of seeing Baba's Hand in the adversity. We can view everyone as "spiritual beings really seeking God." It destroys all sense of injustice to practice seeing everyone, including oneself as reflections of our Beloved God. It also helps us on our way to claiming our True Self.

Gently Down the Stream

By Cynthia Barrientos

While considering surrender with Meher Baba, memories with clarity surfaced from early childhood through recent events. These reflections offer examples that I attribute to being gradually awakened to Baba's love. Each moment of awakening from Baba, combined with conscious acts of surrender, bring me closer and closer to His Ocean of Love.

This first memory highlights this spiritual journey on the stream to the sea. On Christmas Eve, my family had a tradition of us each offering a gift to Baby Jesus. As a three year old, my gift was to sing this English nursery rhyme dating back to the 1800s:

"Row, row, row your boat,
Gently down the stream.
Merrily, merrily, merrily, merrily.
Life is but a dream."

In recent years, I realized how this song illustrates my life with Meher Baba and was my first arti of offering my devotion to Him as Jesus.

- "Row, row, row your boat" is my active participation on this spiritual journey.
- "Gently down the stream" is how I row, when I surrender with Baba.
- "Merrily, merrily, merrily, merrily" aligns with Baba's wish to remain cheerful as best we can.
- "Life is but a dream" refers to the notion that life is an illusion and God alone is real.

In later childhood, an idea came to me that whatever I was thinking at the moment of death, would be where I would go. Being raised a Christian, I heard of Jesus, being saved and going to heaven. In addition, I believed that there were other places or that we would come back to earth. When I learned of reincarnation, that made the most sense to me.

These quotes confirm these early childhood musings, as I long to be with Baba now and forever. He often expressed to His mandali ,

> "Take my name when you breathe your last", along with "Neither seek death nor fear it, and when death comes to you it is converted into a stepping stone to the higher life." -Meher Baba

Another noteworthy glimpse of surrender came during my early adolescent years when I suffered from severe anxiety and panic attacks. At one point I was so distressed that I reached out to my mother for comfort or reassurance, informing her that I was terrified of death. She offered where she was on her own journey and stated that, "They say that if you believe in Jesus, you'll be fine". Her tone was not convincing as I later learned that she was studying Judaism and reading books on Eastern thought and religion. To numb my extreme mental anguish, I turned to alcohol and other distractions as I did not have a belief that Jesus could or would relieve my pain. It was not until the day my mother died that my fear of dying was completely removed and has not returned. This story will appear in reflecting upon my first pilgrimage to Meherabad, India.

When I turned 16, I had what I now consider a vision or an awakening from Baba. While sitting in my family's car, waiting for my father's commuter train to arrive, I went into an altered state without the use of any drugs. I was viewing the Earth from a distance and saw it as a prism, much like a mirrored disco ball with tiny triangles. From the upper right of my sight came a beam of pure white Light that I recognized as God. When the Light touched the Earth, a full spectrum of colors reflected off the prism's facets. I was awakened to the fact that each person, race, religion, culture and country was touched by God, though each experienced it through a different lens of color. I heard the arguments of religion that, "God is red!" with the next one stating that "God is orange!" and the next with, "God is yellow!" and so on. The realization came to me that all were right from how each saw and was touched by God. When we see our world from a distance, we can see God's pure white Light as well as the way Baba stated, "I shall revitalize all religions and cults, and bring them together like beads on one string." [1]

On my first reading of *God Speaks*, I was stunned to see Rano Gayley's colorful chart that Baba described to her. This captured a slice of what I had seen, heard and was awakened to that afternoon at the train station.

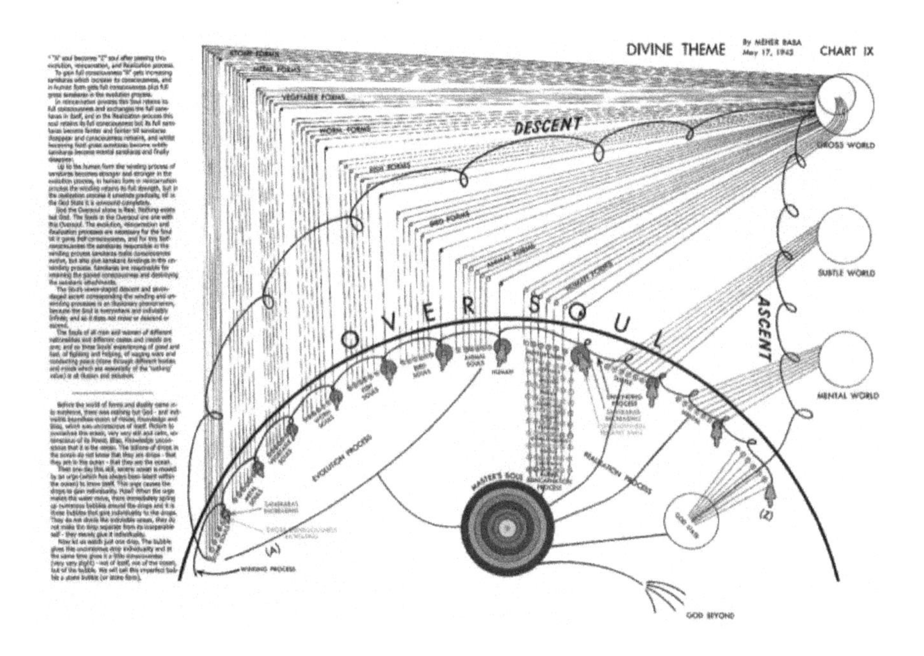

Throughout the remainder of my teens, 20's and 30"s, I was looking for a solution to my anxiety through sex, alcohol, sugar, food, yoga, meditation, self-help books, therapy, work, running and more. Today, I believe that the act was searching was the key to eventual awakening and surrender. Reading a book that had a guide to finding your Spiritual Master, I considered that a spiritual approach may be the solution. Being ready to surrender, I carefully followed the suggestions that included daily meditation to see what name appeared. Sure enough, one day, loud and clear, I heard the name, "Baba". The only Baba I knew of was "Baba Ram Dass' and didn't consider him a Perfect Master, so I simply let go of the whole idea of searching and carried on with my busy life. Little did I know then that I had the first clue to finding Him. When Baba did come to me, I remembered that search and His name.

In 1989, I did find sustainable relief from the many unsuccessful ways I was numbing myself to ease my anxiety. Thanks to a suggested spiritual way of life supported by a fellowship of companions, I have been free of most of these compulsions. Being restored to physical, emotional and spiritual wellness, I believe I was then open and ready to be awakened on a new level by Meher Baba.

During my pregnancy in 1992, I was receiving a massage from a woman who had a photo of Baba by her front door, I would glance at it each time I departed. Most massage therapists I had known had gurus and figured this one was hers. One day I decided to give her a chance to tell me about Him and asked, "Okay. So who is the guy?"

She paused, smiled and said very slowly, "Hmmm... how to describe Meher Baba. He is the One who awakens Love in people's hearts".

My reply was simply, "Cool!" and off I went. That was the extent of our conversation.

Within a few nights, Baba came to me in a dream/vision. The essence of this meeting was that I was awakened to His Love and felt it when He placed His palms together in namasté and invited me to place my hands around His. The sensation I experienced was that of illusion disappearing and not only seeing, though actually FEELING that same Light of God that I saw, though did not feel, as an adolescent that day at the train station. I was IN the Light and felt Love and surrender.

The next day I called my massage therapist and casually informed her, "I dreamed about that guy last night". She got all excited, invited me right over and asked to hear every detail. She then presented dozens of photos of Baba and kept saying, "Did you know that He..." confirming minute details of the dream. My response was always, "How would I know that?" Having only heard His name and seen His image, in the dream/vision, He was at first, very young with long hair and a beard, was walking swiftly, greeted me with namasté, was silent and gestured to communicate. Then, seated in an overstuffed chair with the same brown and white fabric as seen on the cover of Naosherwan Anzar's book, *The Ancient One*, He was older with His hair tied back and His nose was different. The dream ended with me offering Baba strawberry-soy yogurt. He tossed His head back, smiled, looked very happy and offered His gesture of perfection with thumb and index finger connected with three other fingers up. With that, I woke up from the dream and was awakened to Meher Baba.

Thus began my conscious and active surrender with Baba. He continued to visit me while I was sleeping for many months and off and on through the years. Each week, I attended Seattle Baba meetings, read every Baba book I could find, listened to Baba music and watched countless Baba videos. That seemed enough to experience Baba, so I was puzzled and then delightfully surprised when the invitation came for my first pilgrimage in 1994.

That year in January, our local *God Speaks* reading group was planning a five week pilgrimage to Meherabad in November and invited me to come along. My doubtful response was immediate with the reasons of:

#1 being married and a new mom of a 10 month old. The others were single without children.
#2 only two weeks of paid vacation for that year.
#3 no savings to cover the $1100 airfare that needed to be in cash.

My companions smiled and said, "If Baba wants you to come, He will turn the key".

#1 That evening I jokingly presented the invitation to my husband and his instant reply was, "Go for it! We'll be fine. We have great neighbors and extended family. What a great opportunity".

#2 After multiple phone calls with my boss, she insisted the computer displayed three weeks of paid vacation. Being honest, I kept arguing with her and she firmly stated, "Would you just shut up and take it"!

#3 That same week, a hand-signed letter, beginning with, "Dear Cynthia," arrived from the owner of the corporation where I served as an Education Consultant. He said it was a stellar year and decided to now give bonuses to the consultants in addition to the sales team. With this letter was a check for $1100!

Sitting there in my car, with check in hand, I knew that Baba had turned the key and said out loud, “Well, I guess I’m going to India”.

This initial pilgrimage sparked my preparation for what is referred to as Baba “turning up the heat” or that He is “grinding, grinding, grinding” us to become dust at His feet. There was a joke going around that went:

Q: How do you tell the difference between a new baba Lover and an old Baba Lover?
A: The new Baba Lover wants God Realization and the old Baba Lover just wants a day off.

The five weeks in India were clearly the honeymoon, with delightful morning and evening arti, meeting the mandali at Meherazad, road trips to the tombs of Hazarat Babajan, Upasni Maharaj and Sai Baba of Shirdi, connecting with new companions from around the world, daily volleyball in the dust outside the Meher Pilgrim Center (MPC) in lower Meherabad, delicious vegetarian meals, bucket baths with hot water that had the fragrance of wood smoke from how it was heated, an opportunity to drive a bullock cart, shopping for scarves in the Ahmednagar bazaar and most

precious of all, time to sit and be alone with Baba in the Samadhi.

Little did I know that my morning visits with one of Baba's mandali, Mansari, would prepare me for an enormous shock when I returned to Seattle. Each day she would announce that she had filled out her visa to be with Baba and each morning she would wake up and say to us with a twinkle in her eye that, "Baba did not grant me my visa". She seemed happy to be alive and greeting pilgrims in her little room across from the Samadhi and also appeared ready and willing to die and be with Baba once again. Her light-hearted attitude towards dying was intriguing to me with my history of being absolutely terrified of death as a teen and well into my 20"s. Mansari emphasized saying Baba's name at least three times each day so that when we are about to die, His name will be on our lips and we will go to Him. My musings as a child of what we think at the time of death is where we go, now had a clear answer that was comforting for me.

The morning I returned to Seattle, in my exhaustion from hours of travel, I lay down for a nap. After falling into a very deep sleep, I half awoke around 10:30 am, rolled onto my back and witnessed a vision of a figure seated in lotus position and floating up into the same pure white Light I had seen at the train station that day as a teen as well as when Baba came to me and I my hands surrounded His in that first dream/vision.

The words, "I love you!" rose up from my heart to the figure. Looking into what I knew was the Light of God, I repeated with an even deeper feeling of love, "I LOVE You!" Feeling my own spirit begin to float up into the Light, I clearly heard a male voice say, "It's not your turn". My spirit thumped back into my body and I rolled over to return to a dreamless sleep. Around 11:00, the phone rang and my husband said it was for me. I mumbled that I would call them back. He insisted that I take the call. It was my parent's neighbor who was sorry to announce that my mother had just died. In that instant, my fear of death vanished and my faith in Meher Baba became unshakable as I was graced with the honor of witnessing her passing and felt the indescribable Love and Light of God.

This powerful event the day I arrived home from my first pilgrimage was the first in a series of challenging life experiences where I knew that Baba was turning up the heat and my attachment to people, places and things in illusion was in the grinding, grinding, grinding phase. This is where I row, row, row the boat with Baba at my side. As long as I remember Him when faced with internal or external intensity, I can ease into a more gentle way of rowing down the stream, merrily, merrily, merrily, merrily and know that life is but a dream.

Another noteworthy pilgrimage was in 2011 when I was on a long stay of 5 months in India. Early one morning, I had just been trained to clean and prepare Mehera's shrine as the Australian Baba Lover who was to do it was not coming. I overheard that her cancer had returned and she was in Brisbane going through radiation treatments. Then, I clearly heard the deep voice of a woman say, "Go be with her"! I looked around and nobody was close enough to have said that, plus no one there knew that we were friends from previous pilgrimages.

After breakfast, I sent my Australian friend an email, letting her know I had heard the news. In wishing her well on her medical journey, I asked if she had family and friends there with her to offer support. She replied that she was doing this alone. In response I offered to be there with her and her immediate reply was, "Yes!"

When I surrender to a situation that is Baba's will, all details quickly and easily fall into place, much like my first pilgrimage. By noon that same day, I had first class round trip airline tickets to and from Australia using air miles and a visa that was available online for a small fee.

Upon arrival in Brisbane, I described the voice I heard that morning at the Samadhi. She got tears of delight in her eyes and said that the voice was Mehera. She had asked her to send someone and it was me. She had spent a good amount of time with Mehera in her early years with Baba.

The original plan was to stay there for three months, though a family member of mine had a medical emergency back in India and I had to return. Again, Baba turned the key and it was relatively easy to return to Meherabad. Plus, my friend went for her next radiation treatment and the MRI showed no trace of her tumor, so she was able to return to her home many kilometers from Brisbane.

In closing, a final example of surrender in reference to Meher Baba being the Ancient One come again, was being invited to a women's luncheon by a friend who was a devout conservative Christian. I had spoken to her of Meher Baba and she was very worried for me and insisted that Jesus was the only one and the only way to God.

As I sat in the parking lot, all dressed up and ready for the luncheon, I felt resistance to the evangelical nature of her beliefs and practice and considered driving away. Instead, I said out loud to Baba, "If you are here in this church, show me in some way."

About twenty minutes into the event, my phone vibrated with a text. I glanced down to see no words and simply this image of The Ancient One, sent from my spiritual brother, Laurent, author of this book.

Avatar Meher Baba Ki Jai!

P.S. The day after this was submitted, I was beginning to tell my family about this project. I had only gotten as far as saying that it is about surrender with Meher Baba. We were all on the front porch with my six year old grandson, who was playing in our bright green hammock. His voice in song interrupted me, drowning out my words. He sat up, held both sides of the fabric in a rowing motion and belted, "Row, row, row your boat, gently down the stream..." The opening theme of my writing had not yet been spoken, nor did I know he even knew that song. Oh, Baba!

Salt and Pepper

By Geoffrey Wight

Laurent Weichberger reflects in this book that surrender can be and is developed. Meher Baba is explicit in his intention to destroy the limited false mind of his followers and disciples. I confess that as I have a mighty attachment to my mind as self, this intention from Baba is experienced by me as a serious threat to my existence. As I am imbued with a powerful and natural instinct for self-preservation, this is quite the dilemma.

To my surprise, there I am, falling in love with Meher Baba as the Divine Beloved, seeing within me the potential that there might actually exist something called my higher-self. And, I even experience an awakening to the inspiration to be like that. I then have the audacity to embark upon the aspiration to so be; despite my obvious character failings? Still, this threat is simultaneously present, and a fear of the unknown of what would become of me if I surrender. I look for something to hang my disbelieve upon, and Baba's life of contradictions provides me with ample fodder. Meher Baba said to Australian Bill LePage, during the Three Incredible Weeks sahavas in India: "Fear means no love, and love means no fear." But, I do experience both fear and love, and I ask myself, "can fear and love coexist?" I believe perhaps it can.

Having been first introduced to knowledge of Meher Baba in late 1968, a few months before he left this earth plane, it is a time rich with the physical presence of those who had been with Baba, and even lived with and served him as Mandali (his circle of intimate ones). Among those great ones is Margaret Craske, an English ballet mistress from London who lived and travelled with Baba in India from 1939 until 1946, when she moved to the United States. In New York, she taught at the American Ballet Theatre, the Metropolitan Opera Ballet School and at the Manhattan School of Dance. My original career was as a symphonic French horn player, and I experienced a deep, heart felt wish to connect with Margaret Craske, with the commonality of the classical arts, and of course, Meher Baba. Baba has said that he is the slave of the love of his lovers, so as events would happen, I receive an appointment as the General Manager of the Erick Hawkins Dance Company, one of the top five modern dance companies in the world at the time. His studio was on Fifth Avenue, just below 14th Street, on the fifth floor of the building. Well, it so happened that the studio of Margaret Craske was on the third floor. Many times I arrive to work as Margaret is dropped off by taxi, and escort her to her studio, her arm in my arm. What an unbelievable treat.

Around this time, I attend a Baba event at the farm in New Jersey of Elaine Cox where Jal and Dolly Dastur share with us gathered there many stories. Jal speaks of how Baba says he is the slave of the love of his lovers, and that he must fulfill the wish of the heart of his lovers. In this pregnant moment, in the middle of the gathering, these words tumble me backwards into a solitary inner abyss. Sounding my heart's echos, I ask myself, "what is the wish of my heart?" Silently, clearly, calmly, my internal voice sighs with my wish to be able to go to India to put my head at his feet in his Samadhi. Snapping back to my current life reality, I faithlessly think, "that's impossible," as I have just taken a new job, and have no vacation time, nor the money for the trip. On Monday, I sit with the chairman of the company and ask for the time off. Without hesitation, he grants it. And, there is a special, affordable airfare available, so two weeks later I am in India.

Some years pass and I now have a sports related job between the US and India, and am a regular visitor to the Pilgrim Center of Meher Baba. I am finished with my responsibilities and in a taxi from Aurangabad to Ahmednagar, dreamily looking forward to another darshan with Meher Baba at his Samadhi. As the taxi rumbles along, I conjure my wish that brought me to India the first time. So I ask myself, "What is the wish of my heart now?" Again, I enter that mysterious well within that is not about all the doings and appearances that I am so wrapped up in. My echo answer from the depths of this diamond in the (very) rough that I call Geoffrey is that it would be to do night duty at the tomb of Meher Baba. However, I think that is be absolutely impossible, as it was a strict rule that only a resident, one whose home was Ahmednagar, was allowed to do night duty at the tomb. So, I forget about it. Upon arriving to the Pilgrim Center, at about 3:00 in the afternoon, it is time for tea. Sitting down by myself with my hot cup, Peter Booth, a resident American, walks into the dinning hall, comes right over and sits directly across from me. He immediately tells me that the Mandali have given him special permission to offer to a visitor to take his night duty responsibility at the tomb that evening, as he has to go to Bombay. Peter asks me if I would like to do it. Absolutely incredible! I have not spoken a word to anyone of my wish of the heart.

On another visit to India, I am feeling extremely frustrated with the turmoil and confusion I am experiencing, and decide that in such a state, the best place to go is to Baba's Samadhi on the hill. So I take off from the Pilgrim Center, very agitated, frustrated and confused, and angrily think that if I don't get an answer from Baba that I will never again go to the Samadhi. Sensing that I am capable of carrying out an ultimatum, I think to myself as I cross the railroad tracks, this could be the last time that I cross these tracks. And as I walk up the hill, I have a conversation with myself. I ask who do I believe Meher Baba to be, and I respond, "God." And I ask myself, even if I feel totally disappointed with him, who do I believe him to be. The answer, "God." Then I think, in my anger, what can I do? Nothing. Then I think, if I throw away all his books and pictures, will I still love him. Yes. So, now I am still frustrated and angry, but I feel humbled, and perhaps, a bit surrendered. Arriving to the top of the hill, I am drawn to the seclusion hut to the right of the tomb. I sit down on the cool stones and silently have it out with Baba, telling him my frustrations. I hear a voice inside my head. You can say whatever you like about hearing voices, but all I can say is that it did not sound like my regular, internal voice. Here is what the voice says: "If I were you, I'd complain too."

Immediately, I am filled by the sweetest of a bliss, a presence, a love so sublime. It is not "emotional." It cannot be described. It is grace. It is a true gift from God that seems to pour upward from the stone floor, completely entering, surrounding and nourishing the depths of my being. Having been a symphony musician, I know what intense, beautiful emotion is, like performing Beethoven's 9th Symphony in the French horn section. This is so far beyond emotion and imagination that it is to me an undeniable spiritual experience of pure grace. And, I must say, undeserved. In that moment, I realize that my real question is, "Do you love me?" I believed he loved me because he is God, and that's "his job." But, does he really love me, with all my faults, screw ups, mistakes and character flaws? The answer is, yes he does, but not because I was or am worthy.

After some time, what seemed a long time, I am inwardly moved to cross to Baba's tomb and bow down, offering thanks for such a sweet gift. As I put my head at his feet in the Samadhi, I feel as if a hand is pressed on the back of my head, drilling me with the power of God, where before I had experienced the bliss. I feel I could literally die in this moment, and find my mind scrambling to grab ahold of the very frustrations I had just complained of, as that was "me." So, there it is. My ego, my small self, or whatever you want to call it, even when offered a leg-up into that place of heaven on earth, runs to the confusion and chaos. It is familiar. The experience of God's power is scary.

The instant I feel the fear, the power subsides, and I am left with pure bliss. Now, after a long time (again), I decide to leave and go back down the hill where fellow Pilgrims to Meher Baba are finishing breakfast, maybe shaving or taking a morning bath. As I am putting my sneakers on at the bench outside the tomb, again I hear the voice. It says, "That which you seek is vouchsafed in time. Now forget this and live life." I have to confess that in the years to come, I had perhaps a much too liberal interpretation of that, which led to considerable trouble and unnecessary difficulties. But again, the confusion and chaos is familiar.

So the questions is, do I really want God, to be united with my higher, true self, or am I content to throw Meher Baba an occasional "bone" of surrender, here and there, when I am in the mood or it's safe to do so? No real threat in the moment. A moment where I can create the sense that, yes, I am on the spiritual path. But, am I really?

This is what Meher Baba has to say about this.

> "Love has no limit, but the mind is in the way. This obstacle cannot be removed without my grace. It is impossible, because mind has to annihilate itself. For example, if one were asked to jump over oneself, the most one could do would be to take a somersault! Yet it is impossible to jump over oneself; one may jump over others, but not over oneself! Thus one may want to realize "Baba" as he really is, but the obstacle remains.
>
> Books and discourses will not bring about one's spiritual regeneration. Mind cannot be annihilated by mind, for one cannot jump over oneself. Only by loving me as I ought to be loved, can the mind be destroyed. Anyone may have love for me, but not the love I want.
>
> My lovers may be likened to one who is fond of lions and admires them so much that he keeps a lion in his own home. But being afraid of the lion he puts him in a cage. The lion is always encaged; even while he feeds the lion, he feeds the pet animal from a distance and from outside the cage. Baba is treated like the lion by the lovers. There is love; there is admiration; there is an intense desire to see Baba comfortable and happy; and Baba is also frequently fed by love of the lovers. But all this is done, keeping Baba segregated from one's own self.
>
> What is wanted of the lovers is that they should open the "cage" and, through intense love, throw themselves inside the cage to become

> food for the lion of love. The lover should permit himself to be totally consumed through his own love for the Beloved.
>
> In spite of all explanations and reading of books, words remain mere words. They do not take one any further than intellectual satisfaction. Only love for God works the miracle, because love is beyond mind and reason. Where then is the necessity to read? I authoritatively say: I am the Ancient One. I have been saying this to all the world. If you love me with all your heart, you shall be made free eternally."

Meher Baba repeatedly admonishes us to "hold onto my damaan." His damaan being like the skirt of a mother, and me being like the child, clutching to momma's skirt in the confusion and chaos of the market as she goes about her work, so that I am not lost in the throng. To me, Meher Baba's damaan are his words, even though he says "words remain mere words." Yes, that is true, unless acted upon and made real in my walk to the truth. Then words no longer remain mere words. They are alive. Murshida Ivy Duce of Sufism Reoriented years ago admonished me to read Meher Baba's *Discourses* every day, even if just a few paragraphs, saying that Baba's words are not just words, "they are words of light." In Meher Baba's Universal Message he states, in his words, that "I lay down no precepts," and that we have ignored his precepts, his words, throughout eternity, He, again, this time in his silence, has widely cast his damaan in his words, and I have but to read them and let them plant themselves as seeds in me, surrendering in trust that these Divine seeds will somehow take root. Proverbs 8:22-23 lays it out, speaking of Wisdom. "The LORD brought me (wisdom) forth as the first of his works, before his deeds of old; I was formed long ages ago, at the very beginning, when the world came to be."

I have been feeding the Divine Beloved safely in a cage all my life. And, I am most grateful to learn from Laurent Weichberger's work that Baba, most graciously, acknowledges that total surrender to the Master is not possible for all, and provides me with the seven "High Roads."

Meher Baba says,

> "The only REAL SURRENDER is that in which the poise is undisturbed by any adverse circumstance, and the individual, amidst every kind of hardship, is resigned with perfect calm to the will of God."

The High Roads give me an out, the beauty to live with the impossibility of true surrender, and to remain enthusiastic that I have the opportunity to grow in surrender, yet not all at once. To stretch, but not tear, to be challenged, yet not overwhelmed.

Inspired by reading Laurent's latest work, I am taking up re-reading the *Discourses*. Some 52 years after hearing of Meher Baba and experiencing what can be called "his presence," perhaps I have slipped a bit into the valleys of worldly habit, and being reminded to "take up my bed and walk" fills me with fresh excitement.

The eight chapters on meditation in the *Discourses* are an exquisite weave of potential growth, like a personal manual to cut through my individual ignorance. Also, in the last paragraph of Meher baba's Universal Message, what he says, "All this world confusion and chaos was inevitable, and no one is to blame" is a tremendous gift. Baba cuts to the chase. The way I see it, the bottom line is we are all confused, and in chaos. It is not just "out there," it is in my home, my relationships, my family, my life, work, thinking and, yes, in my relationship with Meher Baba. When I wake up to this, I feel I have a start, a possibility. The opposite of confusion is clarity. The opposite of chaos is order. So, if I can begin to understand how things work, the principles behind things, the "laws," I can move and advance. Baba talks about "effort." This spiritual journey, the elimination of our ignorance, takes effort beyond, beyond. As a mater of reference, check out the documentary "Unstoppable" on Bethany Hamilton, the surfer whom a giant tiger shark bit off her left arm at age 13, and she still went on to be a one-armed, world champion surfer. EFFORT! And that is for an achievement in this world. As I surrender, there is effort, simultaneous with letting go. As my surrender grows and increases, so too must my effort.

I confess that Meher Baba's description of himself as the Ancient One, and his masterful revealing of how truly massive is our divine destiny, continues to confound me with its enormity. It is incomprehensible to me, and I struggle to imagine how the Ocean of Existence could be poured into the vessel of the body of Meher Baba. I also marvel at the trail of breadcrumbs, through his words, that he has left for me to follow to this impossibility.

Realizing the impossibility of my really surrendering, I feel I can still offer up myself, good and bad, and that his love is so great that he accepts my offerings as if I were to really surrender. From Proverbs, 20:24: "A person's steps are directed by the LORD. How then can anyone understand their own way?" So, I can surrender to the greatness of his love, even though I may not feel it but here and there.

Reading *Surrender with Meher Baba* has reignited my thirst for the droplets of his love. To me, this book is not for the faint hearted or the weak. It is Meher Baba as the lion that he is. I fear him. I hear his growls. I see him pacing, staring at me through the bars. The question remains, am I willing to enter the cage with him, or better still, release him into my life, to stalk me in every moment, hungry to devour me into the infinity of His love and bliss? Can I really surrender totally to the will of God, with poise and calm? Proverbs, 16:3: "Commit to the LORD whatever you do, and he will establish your plans." Stay tuned..."let them begin...the beguine."

How Long

By Tracey Schmidt

In this garden of Your making
I am weeping.
My loneliness knows no bounds-
And You, hidden at every turn.
What is beauty without You near?
Only grace can dust my lips with color, and bring
Brightness back to my eyes.

I have been given everything, and yet, I am parched and broken.

Like a bird who has forgotten
How to fly, I am.
Like a rose with no fragrance
I have become.

"Come back," you say.
But I am frightened you may ask too much,
Or take everything I have mounted into my sack.

"Return," You say.
I glance at the place where I once wore Your ring,
Its imprint still shows upon my finger.

"Surrender," You say.
And suddenly the gate swings open
To the inner courtyard
Where You have been, Baba, all along-
The moon a reflection of my sorrow,
for how long I have been away from
You.

Epilogue

by Vanessa Weichberger

What might be keeping you from surrender?

Surrender is about your relationship with God, and forgiveness is about your relationship with yourself.

As you surrender, which is basically surrendering the ego, you grow in love. The only thing we have to give the master is our ego, that's why he says give me your weaknesses, right?

Surrender takes you beyond what you understand to be "right" or "wrong." Surrender inspires the grace of the master. Surrender is a great leap of faith. You must walk into the nothing, where nothing is known to find everything. It's like asking to be blinded to find the light. The ego holds onto its own darkness by asserting "what is, what could be, would be, can be, should be, or must be." It is in the act of letting all of these stories go that one walks into the nothing, where suddenly there is the everything. In that everything, that infinite space, is the experience of "I am" – that needs nothing, desires nothing. In that desirelessness we find the peace and fulfillment we could never find in having our story.

The bait is love.
The trap is love.

In the end we are all in the world of illusion until we reach the goal of union with our beloved. Therefore the very experience of right or a wrong is also an illusion. To engage with right or wrong only perpetuates it. When I said "bait and trap" it is the very illusion which baits us into engaging with it and when entrenched or "trapped" in this illusion it is the distaste of its effects which brings us to the point of surrender or, "no longer identifying or engaging in it." Thus, the only real pursuit is the pursuit of the one truth which is our path to union with God, as he is the one truth. Until that union comes to pass, Meher Baba gave us the following guidance:

> "To penetrate into the essence of all being and significance, and to release the fragrance of that inner attainment for the guidance and benefit of others, by expressing in the world of forms truth, love, purity and beauty – this is the sole game which has any intrinsic and absolute worth. All other happenings, incidents and attainments in themselves can have no lasting importance."

When we detach from the illusion, we gain freedom and the ability to love without expectation of results or circumstances. It becomes a joy just to love regardless of the outcome. Love becomes the spontaneous and selfless reality. With that in mind, it leads us to the following seven realities which, as one practices surrender, become the outcome of its intangible but very real presence in our lives:

The Seven Realities of Meher Baba's Teaching

Meher Baba's teaching gives no importance to creed, dogma, caste systems and the performance of religious ceremonies and rites, but to the understanding of the following seven realities: [1]

1. The only Real Existence is that of the One and only God, who is the Self in every (finite) self.

2. The only Real Love is the love for this Infinity (God), which arouses an intense longing to see, know and become one with its Truth (God).

3. The only Real Sacrifice is that in which, in pursuance of this love, all things, body, mind, position, welfare and even life itself, are sacrificed.

4. The only Real Renunciation is that which abandons, even in the midst of worldly duties, all selfish thoughts and desires.

5. The only Real Knowledge is the knowledge that God is the inner dweller in good people and so-called bad, in saint and so-called sinner. This knowledge requires you to help all equally as

circumstances demand, without expectation of reward, and when compelled to take part in a dispute, to act without the slightest trace of enmity or hatred; to try to make others happy, with brotherly or sisterly feeling for each one; to harm no one in thought, word or deed, not even those who harm you.

6. The only Real Control is the discipline of the senses from indulgence in low desires, which alone ensures absolute purity of character.

7. The only Real Surrender is that in which the poise is undisturbed by any adverse circumstances, and the individual, amidst every kind of hardship, is resigned with perfect calm to the will of God.

Avatar Meher Baba Ki Jai!

About the Authors

Merwan S. Irani was born to Persian Zoroastrian parents in Pune India in 1894. His parents were both Iranian and settled in India. He experienced spiritual enlightenment as a young man during his college days, through an encounter with Hazrat Babajan, the great Sufi master. He became known as a spiritual master, and his early disciples named him Meher Baba which means compassionate one. He proclaimed himself "The Avatar of the Age," and he moved to an abandoned British military camp near the remote village of Arangaon where he lived with his twelve Mandali (disciples). This initial residence is called Meherabad. He also built a residence called Meherazad where he lived until his passing in 1969. Baba has many followers from all over the world as well as Indian devotees. For his spiritual work, he chose to remain silent at the age of 31, in 1925, and he remained silent until his death. He spent his life in service, helping those in need. He was especially focused on helping lepers and also masts, who are individuals that are "God intoxicated" and therefore have trouble functioning on the earthly plane.

Meher Baba first came to the United States in 1931, and with the help of his western followers, he built a universal spiritual retreat center in Myrtle Beach, South Carolina. This Center served as his "Home in the West," and it is still an active retreat center where his followers from all over the world can visit and commune with Baba. There are many documentary films that have been made about Baba and his life, and the Baba center has an extensive library that includes these films as well as numerous writings by Baba and his Mandali. There are also many volumes of spiritual writings from all faiths.

- by Sarah Weichberger

Don Stevens was one of Meher Baba's early Western followers and he became one of Baba's inner circle. Don met Baba in 1952, in New York City. Meher Baba considered Don one of his Mandali, even though he wasn't living in India. Don spent most of his life after meeting Baba working on writing projects given to him by Baba, including *God Speaks*, *Listen, Humanity*, and *Discourses* (6th ed. three volumes). He was also a career executive at Standard Oil of California, (which later became Chevron and other companies). Don passed away in London during 2011, at the age of 92.

Evie Lindemann, ATR-BC, ATCS, LMFT, is a licensed marriage & family therapist and a board certified art therapist, and until recently she has been an Associate Professor in the Master of Arts in Art Therapy and Counseling Program at Albertus Magnus College. She also taught at Yale University's Sherwin B. Nuland Summer Institute of Bioethics for seven years. Deeply influenced by the teachings of Meher Baba, Evie has lived and worked in Afghanistan, Israel, and India. She has implemented humanitarian art therapy projects in India, Jamaica, and the US. She is active in hospice care, teaches courses on mortality, and uses the visual arts to facilitate the inward journey. Additionally, she has worked with combat veterans who have complex trauma, using art therapy as a modality for healing. She has studied the Jungian tradition extensively and is certified as an Archetypal Pattern Analyst. She is a printmaking artist whose work has been exhibited nationally and internationally. For some years, Evie has worked with mandalas as a symbol of wholeness, has taught a system of symbols and colors (the MARI) to clinicians around the world, and offers consultations to individuals and groups interested in depth exploration using the MARI as a tool of integration.

Tracey Schmidt's first book of poetry *I Have Fallen in Love* with the World, was written mostly at the Center and is available on Amazon. She has a museum touring photography exhibit about native Americans called

"The Awakening of Turtle Island: Portraits of Native People." "More here: www.traceyschmidt.com or www.traceyschmidt/poetry.com
She lives in Asheville with two hives of bees and a white turtle dove. She has fallen in love with the world. She's still not sure how that happened.

Daniel Stone became a Baba-lover in 1972 and founded the Meher Baba Washington Gathering along with Kitty Davy in 1976. For many years he has been writing, presenting, and consulting to Baba groups around the world. Daniel has a private practice as an organizational change consultant. He is also a musician, having released a CD in 2018 entitled "*Decorate with Song.*" Currently Daniel lives in Myrtle Beach, where he serves on the board of directors for the Meher Spiritual Center.

For the past four years, **Tom Wolfe** has been Clerk of Ministry and Worship at Annapolis Friends (Quaker) Meeting in Annapolis Maryland. Tom is also clerk of "Be Friendly Ministries", an embraced Quaker Ministry held by Annapolis Friends Meeting. The mission of Be Friendly Ministries is to show specifically how God's message has been faithful and consistent for six thousand years, from Zarathustra to Jesus onward to Meher Baba. This work will use the method of William Penn, perfected in 1668 showing three of the world's religions (Christianity, Islam, and Judaism) clearly to be Beads On a Single String. With thirty three principles of Meher Baba, Be Friendly Ministries will expand Penn's Beads On a Single String work to twelve faiths which represent 82 percent of the current world's population. Be Friendly Ministries is on track to publish its first title, *33 Ways 7 Other Religions Agree with Meher Baba.* BeFriendlyMinistries.org to keep in touch.

Cyprus Weichberger: I am in 8th grade, I love athletics, creativity, and just having fun. I enjoy vacation, the ocean, and talking to people. I want to be a successful rapper some day so this is the beginning of my long journey. My Instagram is cbreez111 and my email is: cyprusweichberger@gmail.com. If you want to be a part of my journey then let me know. Until then live life to fulfill your wishes and make others happy, because you never know when you'll get to do it again.

Cynthia Barrientos was born and raised in the San Francisco Bay Area and migrated north to the Pacific Northwest in the 1970s. She was awakened to Avatar Meher Baba's Love in November of 1992, in her Seattle, Washington home. Shortly after seeing His photo and hearing His name, He visited her while she was sleeping. This was the first of many awakenings presented in her upcoming book, *Awakened In the Night.* With Meher Baba as her constant companion, her creativity as a writer has flourished in publications including *The Love Street Lamp Post, OmPoint International Circular*, and *Heart Chronicles*. Available later this year, *The Meher Baba Alphabet Book* depicts Beloved Meher Baba with playful couplets and beautiful, colorful images of Him from artists around the world.

Alan Manoukian lives in California with his wonderful wife and elderly cat. You can check out his blog with more Baba stories at: www.avatarmeherbaba.tumblr.com

Geoff Wight is married to Licia, and enjoys two children, daughter Francesca, 19 and son, Alexander 29. Living in southern Florida in the "Winter Equestrian Capital of the World," provides a continuous opportunity to be reminded of the love for horses that Meher Baba's dear one, Mehera, knew and expressed. Of the high roads, number 6 is his challenge.: "Carrying on all worldly duties with a pure heart and clean mind and with equal acceptance of success or failure, while remaining detached in the midst of intense activity."

Laurent Weichberger came to follow Meher Baba in Manhattan during 1986. His first publication for Baba was, *A Mirage Will Never Quench Your Thirst: A Source of Wisdom about Drugs,* aimed at helping the youth of America to stop using drugs, and to find a natural high through the life of the spirit. That project connected him with Don Stevens, and they worked together for Baba from 2002 until Don's passing nine years later. During that time, Don asked Laurent to help a specific Baba group with forgiveness, which resulted in a seminar series, "Forgiveness with Meher Baba," and a book of the same title. The forgiveness work spawned an urge to apply a similar approach with surrender. The seminar Surrender with Meher Baba was created, which evolved into this volume. Laurent is an IT consultant specializing in Big Data technologies, as well as Blockchain. He lives in North Carolina with his wife, children, and Khadija their loving Korat.

Endnotes by Chapter

Chapter One: Opening

[1] *Mehera-Meher, A Divine Romance*, by David Fenster, Vol. 3, pp. 509-510.

[2] *Lord Meher*, p. 4441 (accessed Sept. 2019),
See also: The Everything and the Nothing, by Meher Baba, p. 64

[3] See: https://www.merriam-webster.com/dictionary/surrender

[4] With all due respect to other spiritual paths which have other foci, such as the path of knowledge, or the path of service, or any other path.

[5] Psalms of David, 46:10.

[6] See also https://en.wikipedia.org/wiki/1964_New_York_World%27s_Fair. The photo was selected by Baba for this message.

[7] From the message, "My Dear Workers," in The 1962 East-West Gathering, pp. 4-9.

Chapter Two: The Meaning of Surrender

[1] From a poem titled, "Holy is Your Name," *Stranger Music: Selected Music and Songs*, by Leonard Cohen, p. 331 (Vintage Books, 1994).

[2] *Discourses*, by Meher Baba Vol. II, p. 183.

[3] *Leonard Cohen on Leonard Cohen*, edited by Jeff Burger (Chicago: Chicago Review Press, 2015), p. 166, from an interview during December 1984. See also: https://en.wikipedia.org/wiki/Leonard_Cohen

[4] See: https://en.wikipedia.org/wiki/Lord"s_Prayer

[5] See: New Testament, "Gospel of Luke," chapter 22, verse 42. On-line: http://web.mit.edu/jywang/www/cef/Bible/NIV/NIV_Bible/LUKE+22.html

[6] [Ibid, "Gospel of John." chapter 10, verse 30.]

Chapter Three: Divine Right Timing

[1] *Lord Meher* online p. 5142

[2] *Lord Meher* online p. 5058

[3] *Ramayana*, by William Buck (Aleph Book Company, 2019).

[4] *Lord Meher* online p. 4757

[5] Ibid on-line p. 4024]

[6] *Lord Meher*, p. 2810, on-line. See also, Meher Baba's New Life, pp. 156-157, by V.S. "Bhau" Kalchuri.

[7] *The Little Flowers of St. Francis*, edited by Raphael Brown (Image Books, 1971).

[8] *Ibid*, p. 4025, on-line: http://www.lordmeher.org/rev/index.jsp?pageBase=page.jsp&nextPage=4025

Chapter Four: The Gift

[0] *Discourses*, Vol II pg. 74, "The Nature of the Ego and its Termination: II"

[1] *God Speaks*, by Meher Baba (Dodd Mead reprint, 1997) See also: www.amazon.com/God-Speaks-Meher-Baba/dp/0915828022/

[2] *Discourses*, "The Removal of Sanskaras: III," (Vol. I, p. 89)

[3] *Discourses*, "The Nature of the Ego and its Termination," (Volume II, pp. 74 & 78)

[4] In the booklet, *Meher Baba's Call.*

[5] *Discourses by Meher Baba*, From "The Dynamics of Spiritual Advancement," (Vol. II, p. 183.)

[6] *God Speaks*, by Meher Baba (Walnut Creek: Sufism Reoriented, 1973) p. 137.

[7] *The Essential Rumi*, by Coleman Barks (Castle Books, 1997).

[8] One of the books is titled, *God is Red*, by Vine Deloria, Jr. (Fulcrum Publishing, 2003).

[9] An anonymous elder was noted as having shared this poetic prophecy at the Oraibi, Arizona Hopi Nation. See also: http://www.twohawks.com/hopi/

Chapter Five: Passive Versus Active Surrender

[1] The seminar, "Obedience and Surrender with Meher Baba," was conducted at the home of Jennifer Tinsman and Paul DiStefano, in Myrtle

Beach, South Carolina. Daniel Stone facilitated the first session on Obedience.

[2] *Lord Meher*, p. 2154 on-line: http://www.lordmeher.org/rev/index.jsp?pageBase=page.jsp&nextPage=2154

Chapter Six: Healthy, Deficient, and Toxic Surrender

[1] *Discourses*, by Meher Baba, Volume 3, p. 181, on-line here: https://discoursesbymeherbaba.org/v3-181.php

Chapter Seven: Evolutionary Resistance to Surrender

[1] Lord Meher, p. 1961 online: http://www.lordmeher.org/rev/index.jsp?pageBase=page.jsp&nextPage=1961 (accessed April 2020). Ms. Margaret Craske, from the West, joined them after this initial departure.

[2] *Discourses*, "Maya: II," p. 13 by Meher Baba.

Chapter Eight: Surrender and Separation

[1] Version by Kabir Helminski in, *The Rumi Collection: An Anthology of Translations and Versions of Jalaluddin Rumi* (Putney, Vermont: Threshold Books, 1998), pp. 145-46. This is a revision of earlier versions (*Love is A Stranger*, 1993, pp. 50-52; *Ruins of the Heart*, 1981, pp. 19-20).

[2] Translation by Azita Namiranian and Laurent Weichberger (October 12, 2019). Original in, *The Divan of Hafiz*, compiled and edited by Ismail Salami (*Tehran: Arena of Persian Art & Thought*, 2011). Farsi provided here.

[3] In, *Listen, Humanity*, by Meher Baba (ed. Don E. Stevens) pp. 17-18.

[4] Translation November 2019 by Azita with Vanessa and Laurent. Originally in, *The Divan of Hafiz*, compiled and edited by Ismail Salami (*Tehran: Arena of Persian Art & Thought*, 2011).

Chapter Nine: Surrender Anecdotes

[1] As I write this paragraph, the Leonard Cohen song "Hallelujah" just started to play on the radio in the restaurant here in Charlotte where I am writing. Hallelujah can be translated as, "Sing God's praise." See: https://genius.com/Leonard-cohen-hallelujah-lyrics

[2] From my notes October 18, 2017 which Dr. Rose reviewed, corrected, and approved.

[3] Cynthia Griffin further shared, "Meher Baba's twin nephews came to our house and they stated it was given (written) to them by Mani." She confirmed the content of the quote via email to me September 7, 2017.

Chapter Ten: Surrender with Meher Baba

[1] *Lord Meher* online, p. 3560, here: http://www.lordmeher.org/rev/index.jsp?pageBase=page.jsp&nextPage=3560 "In all honesty, I was not there. When I use quotes to describe this exchange it is based on my memory of how Don describe:d this to me. Please don't take this too literally. This is this gist of what Don said to me."

[2] This was my Feb 25, 2020 commentary about these Baba quotes for Surrender with Meher Baba (on a plane from Wilmington to Dallas, TX). There are so many quotes from Baba on surrender that I felt this sample, from material Baba himself approved, was a good way to start. Future generations can do a more exhaustive search and compile all we have on this subject from beloved Baba.

[3] *Lord Meher*, on-line edition, p. 663, (accessed March 2020) here:]

[4] See: https://en.wikipedia.org/wiki/Mother_Teresa

[5] These quotes are from the book: *Listen, Humanity* (hereafter "LH") which we used in PDF form as "*Listen, Humanity*.pdf" page numbers are based on the PDF page numbers. LH, p. 16. I have normalized the word "sahvas' to "sahavas' which is how we now use it in the Meher Baba community.

[6] Ibid, p. 21]
[7] [Ibid, p. 124]
[8] [Ibid, pp. 124-125]
[9] [Ibid, p. 125]
[10] [Ibid, p.125]
[11] [Ibid, pp. 125-126]
[12] [Ibid, p. 137]
[13] [Ibid, p. 158]
[14] [Ibid, p. 163]
[15] [Ibid, p. 164]
[16] [Ibid, p. 165]

[17] See: https://www.meherbabatravels.com/his-close-ones/men/lyn-ott/

[18] [Ibid, p. 178]
[19] [Ibid, p. 189]
[20] [Ibid, p. 190]
[21] [Ibid, p. 190]
[22] [Ibid, p. 191]
[23] [Ibid, p. 193]

[24] September 6, 1953 as told in, *Lord Meher*, p. 3391 on-line: http://www.lordmeher.org/rev/index.jsp?pageBase=page.jsp&nextPage=3391

[25] *Listen, Humanity*, p. 229. This is also part of the message, "The Highest of the High."

[26] Ibid, pp. 229-230. This is also part of the message, "The Highest of the High."]

[27] [Ibid, p. 231. This is also part of the message, "The Highest of the High."]

[28] See also: https://en.wikipedia.org/wiki/Trauma_trigger.

[29] See also: https://thichnhathanhfoundation.org/.

[30] See also: https://en.wikipedia.org/wiki/Triune_brain.

[31] Ibid, p. 239. This is the first part of a message: "Directions Given by Meher Baba, November 1955, Particularly for the participants of the sahavas weeks, and in general for all connected with Baba."

[32] [Ibid, p. 241]

Chapter Eleven: Surrender in Song

[1] *Bhagavad-Gita* is the holy scripture of Hinduism in which Krishna reveals the Truth to his close disciple Arjuna. Christian hymn lyrics by Frances Ridley Havergal (1836-1879).

[2] From the music album *Open Up the Door*, copyright © 2020 by Buz Connor, used by permission. The lyrics from the chorus "I must do my best to lay it down and let my Father take over," were written by Lee Rogers Minchey. Lyrics transcribed by Cyprus Weichberger.

Chapter Twelve: Surrender and Wellbeing

[1] Sangha is literally: "The Buddhist community of monks, nuns, novices, and laity."

[2] From Julie in Sedona Arizona, via email: March 18, 2020 5:33am. DMQ means Doctor of Medical Qigong therapy.

[3] In the book, *Discourses*, by Meher Baba, see http://discoursesbymeherbaba.org/v1-16.php and https://www.avatarmeherbaba.org/erics/7realities.html, see also: Lord Meher, volume 7-8, p. 2654. It was dictated by Meher Baba in Jaipur, India on Thursday, January 9, 1941.

[4] *The God-Man*, by Charles Purdom, p. 320

Chapter Thirteen: Experience

[1] *The Doorbell of Forgiveness*, by Don E. Stevens, with his young people's group (London: Companion Books, 2011).

[2] *Meditation: A Simple Eight-Point Program for Translating Spiritual Ideals into Daily Life*, by Eknath Easwaran (Nilgiri Press).

Chapter Sixteen: Alan Manoukian

[1] *Glow International*, May 1985 p.1.

[2] *Listen, Humanity*, p.158.

[3] Ibid, p.158

Chapter Nineteen: Thomas Wolfe

[1] Meher Baba, *Discourses*, 7th edition. P. 46.

[2] *The Divine Songs of Zarathustra*. Ustavaiti 4:17–Yasna 46:17.

[3] *Bhagavad Gita*. 4.20.

[4] *Bhagavad Gita*. 5.12.

[5] *Tanakh: The Holy Scriptures*. Isaiah 43:2–3.

[6] *The Dhammapada*. 6:83.

[7] *The New Testament,* "Matthew," 7:21 (AV).

[8] *The Qur"an*, "Al-Baqarah (The Cow)," 2:153–156.

[9] *The Qur"an,* "ʾIbrãhĩm (Abraham)," 14:12.

[10] William Penn, 21st Century Penn: *Writings on the Faith and Practice of the People Called Quakers*, 1694. (Richmond, Indiana: Earlham School of Religion Press, 2003), p. 364.

[11] Meher Baba, *Discourses*, 7th edition. P. 148.

[12] Meher Baba, *Discourses*, 7th edition. P. 257.

[13] *The Divine Songs of Zarathushtra*. Spenta-Mainyu 3.5–Yasna 49.5.

[14] *Bhagavad Gita*. 4.20.

[15] *Bhagavad Gita.* 12.20.

[16] *Tanakh: The Holy Scripture*. 2 Chronicles 30:8–9.

[17] *The Dhammapada*. 7:96.

[18] *The New Testament*, "Matthew," 7:21 (AV).

[19] *The Qur'an.* "Al-Baqarah (The Cow)," 2:112.

[20] *The Qur'an*, "ʾĀl-ʿImrān ," 3:19–20.

[21] John Woolman's last words, 1772, *The Journal of John Woolman* (HC). P. 314.

[22] Meher Baba, *Listen Humanity* p.144

[23] Meher Baba from the message: "*The Highest of the High.*"

Chapter Twenty: Daniel J. Stone

[1] "*Everything and the Nothing*", Meher Baba, page 64

[2] As told to Naosherwan Anzar by Arnavaz Dadachanji

[3] As soon as the accident happened, Adi looked at his watch, and saw that it was exactly 12 noon

[4] "*Love Alone Prevails*", Kitty Davy, page 304

[5] "*Discourses*", Meher Baba, 7th Edition, pages 58-59

[6] For a full description of these New Life meetings, see "*Lord Meher*" by Bhau Kalchuri, beginning page 2739 of the online edition

[7] *"The Joyous Path"*, Heather Nadel, page 101

[8] from a talk by Naosherwan entitled "In God's Hand", available on YouTube

[9] "Slave of Love", Bob Mossman, page 159

[10] "The God Man" by C. B. Purdom, page 320

[11] *Love Alone Prevails"*, Kitty Davy, page 167

[12] "*God Speaks*", Meher Baba, page xxxvi

[13] *Lord Meher* Volumes 11 and 12, page 3812

[14] Just prior to dropping His body on January 31, 1969, Baba had three couplets of Hafiz read out: "Befitting a fortunate slave, carry out every command of the Master without any question of why and what; about what you hear from the Master, never say it is wrong because, my dear, the fault lies in your own incapacity to understand Him; I am the slave of my Master, who has released me from ignorance; whatever my Master does is of the highest benefit to all concerned." Mehera commented on this, saying, "This is His [final] message to us." ("*Mehera-Meher*", David Fenster, Volume III, page 510)

[15] *Discourses*, 7th edition, p. 44

[16] "*Life at Its Best*", Meher Baba, page 26

Chapter Twenty Two: Cynthia Barrientos

[1] *God Speaks*, by Meher Baba, p. xxxvi 1973

Vanessa Weichberger: Epilogue

[1] *Discourses*, Volume I, p.15. On-line: https://discoursesbymeherbaba.org/v1-15.php

Acknowledgements

First and foremost, all my love and profound respect for my amazing wife Vanessa. You have come so far, and your voice is now clear and powerful -- a tool for Baba's healing in the world. As Mani said, an example for the West. You are that. I love you my Halime Sultan, thank you for supporting my life's work in all the ways you do. May Beloved Baba help you to surrender also.

All my soul for my Beloved Avatar Meher Baba, you have received my surrender, and encourage me ever onward with your Real Love.
My gratitude for my dear mother Anne, and splendid sister Sarah, for bringing me into the world, and helping me grow up in so many ways. We three have had our fair share of opportunities to surrender, eh?

To all the contributing authors, Cynthia, Tracey, Evie, Dale, Alan, Daniel, Thomas, Geoff, Vanessa, and Cyprus my spiritual companions, my family, on the Way back to Beloved Baba. I love and respect you all so deeply, and I'm so glad you shared the nectar of your heart and mind here with us all.

I bow to you my dearest daughter, and editor, Aspen, for asking me to be more vulnerable in my writing, and holding my feet to the fire. Your editing, encouragement, and guidance on these last two books mean so much to me, and I love working with you. I love you more than space, and...

Salaam, Karl Moeller. You have done an amazing job on all the work we have done together for Baba, too many things to list, and I thank you. I have full faith in you once again. Let's keep at it man, all for him.

Hugh Flick, you have gone above and beyond as a proofreader and editor, and now I am indebted to you, my Baba-brother.

And lastly, I wish to thank Mr. Preetpal Singh, my current boss. You and I are cut from the same divine cloth, my hero. You responded to my prayers, and my surrender. May God bless you.

Suggested Further Reading

Discourses, by Meher Baba, Revised 6th Edition (Myrtle Beach: Sheriar Foundation, 2007) ~ 904p. sheriarbooks.org

God Speaks, by Meher Baba (2nd edition, 1973) ~ 313p. sheriarbooks.org

The Divan of Hafiz (English - Persian), by Hafiz, translated by Ismail Salami (Tehran: Gooya House of Culture and Art, 2003) ~ 516p. amazon.com/Divan-Hafiz-English-Illuminated-Manuscript/dp/B001TEWBTO

A Mirage Will Never Quench Your Thirst: A Source of Wisdom about Drugs, Compiled and edited by Laurent Weichberger & Laura Smith (Myrtle Beach: Sheriar Foundation, 2003) ~ 141p. amazon.com/Mirage-Will-Never-Quench-Thirst/ dp/188061927X/

Related drug article: Ayahuasca This Way Comes, by Laurent Weichberger (Flagstaff: The Noise, 2008): on-line at http://issuu.com/ompoint/docs/ayahuascathiswaycomes

Meher Baba's Word and His Three Bridges, by Don E. Stevens with Norah Moore, and Laurent Weichberger (London: Com- panion Books, 2003) ~ 234p. amazon.com/Meher-Babas-Word-Three-Bridges /dp/0952509741/

Meher Baba's Gift of Intuition, by Don E. Stevens and Compan- ions (London: Companion Books, 2006) ~ 197p. amazon.com/Meher-Babas-Intuition-Stevens- Companions/dp/0952509768/

Celebrating Divine Presence: Journeys into God, by Laurent Weichberger, Yaakov Weintraub, Karl Moeller, et al (London: Companion Books, 2008) ~ 392p. amazon.com/Celebrating-Divine-Presence-Journeys-into/dp/0952509792/

Among The Sleeping: Sufism Within And Without Islam, Karl Moeller (2018) ~ 204p. amazon.com/Among-Sleeping-Sufism-Within-Without /dp/0692064249

The Doorbell of Forgiveness, by Don E. Stevens with his Young People's Group (London: Companion Books, 2011) ~ 290p. amazon.com/ Doorbell-Forgiveness-Don-E-Stevens/dp/095250975X

Three Snapshots of Reality, by Don E. Stevens with Wayne Smith (London: Companion Books, 2014) ~ 133p. amazon.com/Three-Snapshots-Reality-Don-Steve ns/dp/0956553001/

Forgiveness with Meher Baba (4th ed.), by Laurent Weichberger & Companions (Wilmington: OmPoint Press, 2016) - 264 p. amazon.com/ Forgiveness-Meher-Baba-Laurent-Weichberger/dp/0692722572